THE
MUMMY'S
CURSE

Avon Flare Books by
Daniel Cohen

THE BEHEADED FRESHMAN AND OTHER NASTY RUMORS
SOUTHERN FRIED RAT AND OTHER GRUESOME TALES

DANIEL COHEN is a prolific author of more than 150 books for young people and adults. He has written on a wide variety of topics, everything from astronomy to zoology, but is best known for his books on weird and offbeat topics like ghosts, monsters and, of course, creepy legends. He lives with his wife, who is also a writer, three cats, and two Clumber spaniels in Cape May, New Jersey. He is a devotee of the Sherlock Holmes stories and believes that there really was a Sherlock Holmes and that Sir Arthur Conan Doyle was Dr. Watson's literary agent.

THE MUMMY'S CURSE

101 OF THE WORLD'S STRANGEST MYSTERIES

DANIEL COHEN

AN AVON CAMELOT BOOK

THE MUMMY'S CURSE: 101 OF THE WORLD'S STRANGEST MYSTERIES is an original publication of Avon Books. This work has never before appeared in book form.

AVON BOOKS
A division of
The Hearst Corporation
1350 Avenue of the Americas
New York, New York 10019

Copyright © 1994 by Daniel Cohen
Published by arrangement with the author
Library of Congress Catalog Card Number: 94-4378
ISBN: 0-380-77093-8
RL: 5.0

Library of Congress Cataloging in Publication Data:

Cohen, Daniel, 1936–
    101 of the world's strangest mysteries / Daniel Cohen.
        p.   cm.
    1. Curiosities and wonders. I. Title. II. Title: One hundred and one of the world's strangest mysteries.
AG243.C572   1994   94-4378
031.02—dc20   CIP
                                            AC

First Avon Camelot Printing: October 1994

CAMELOT TRADEMARK REG. U.S. PAT. OFF. AND IN OTHER COUNTRIES, MARCA REGISTRADA, HECHO EN U.S.A.

Printed in the U.S.A.

OPM   10   9   8   7   6   5   4

CONTENTS

PART II PLACES

PART III THINGS

INTRODUCTION

The Lure of the Unknown

One possible definition of a human being is "a mystery-loving animal."

To test the accuracy of that observation all one has to do is look at the eternal popularity of fictional sleuths. Real mysteries are endlessly examined and reexamined in books, articles and highly rated TV shows.

I freely admit that I am a glutton for such fare and have been for as long as I can remember. All I have to do is hear that something is mysterious, unexplained or unknown, and I'm hooked. I have been fortunate enough to have been able to spend a good part of my professional career writing about these subjects.

Here is a group of 101 greatest mysteries from all fields: history, science, crime, the occult, you name it.

Oh, I can hear the quibbles already: "Why did you include this one and not that one?" "How about the case of . . . ?" And so on. And the critics are right. All lists are essentially arbitrary. Yours would be different. This list happens to be mine—comprising mysteries that over the years have captured my imagination.

Even if you would not agree that all the selections on the list are among the 101 greatest, I'm sure you will agree that most of them are, and I hope you will find all of them intriguing, exciting and entertaining—above all, entertaining.

Have fun!

I.
People

THE MAN IN THE IRON MASK

The story of a mysterious masked prisoner was made famous in a historical romance novel of the same name written in 1848 by Alexandre Dumas, creator of *The Three Musketeers*. In the novel, the mysterious prisoner is the twin brother of King Louis XIV, who had been imprisoned to save France from a struggle for succession between the two brothers.

As in most of Dumas's historical novels this one freely mixes fact and fancy. A mysterious masked man was really a prisoner during the reign of Louis XIV. And speculation concerning the prisoner's identity has been hardly less fanciful than the novel.

All that is known for certain is that the prisoner was brought to Paris in 1698 by Benigne de Saint-Mars, who had just been named superintendent of the notorious prison, the Bastille. The prisoner was not allowed to communicate with any of the other inmates, and whenever he was seen, he wore a velvet, not an iron, mask. The prisoner died in 1703 and was buried in the cemetery of St. Paul under the name Marchioli. Before the prisoner had been brought to the Bastille he had apparently been in the Pignerol prison in Italy and in a prison on the island of St. Marguerita, near Cannes.

Some fifty years after the prisoner's death, the great French writer Voltaire either originated or popularized the idea that he wore an iron mask. Voltaire was one of the first to speculate that the mystery man was a brother of the king.

Everyone from an illegitimate son of Charles II of England to the French playwright Molière has been advanced as the true identity of the mysterious prisoner. A less exciting but more probable explanation is that he was Count Ercole Antonio Mattioli, a spy. Count Mattioli was known to have been imprisoned at Pignerol and moved several times. He is believed to have died in 1703, the same year as the masked prisoner. And the prisoner, you will recall, was buried under the name Marchioli, close enough to Mattioli. Two of Louis XIV's successors were said to have identified the prisoner as Count Mattioli.

There is, however, a problem with the identification. The details of Count Mattioli's crime and arrest were well known. For a time he was one of the best-known prisoners in France. What need would there be to hide his identity?

Louis XIV. Was his brother the Man in the Iron Mask?

A more intriguing possibility is another prisoner at Pignerol named Eustache Dauger. He had been imprisoned at Pignerol since 1669. Though prison records refer to him only as a servant, from the beginning extraordinary precautions were taken to keep him from talking with other prisoners or anyone but a very few trusted prison officials. Records do not reveal the nature of Dauger's crime or his ultimate fate. But his treatment was certainly unusual.

Some hold that Dauger was the king's half-brother or even his father! Louis XIII and his queen thoroughly disliked one another. After twenty-two years of marriage they failed to produce an heir, and it was whispered the king was impotent. Then a boy who was to become Louis XIV was born to the queen, an event widely described at the time as "a miracle." Could the real father of the baby have been a vigorous young palace servant? There would be good reason to hide the face of the servant or any of his other children if they bore a resemblance to the new king.

This is just the latest twist in nearly three centuries of speculation.

NOSTRADAMUS

Michel de Nostredame, better known by his pen name Nostradamus, was a sixteenth-century French almanac maker and prophet. He is also, by far, the most famous nonbiblical prophet in his and our times. Practically everyone today has at least heard his name. Any new interpretation of his prophecies is likely to attract a lot of believers.

Nostradamus was born on December 14, 1503, at St. Remy, in Provence. He started his career as a physician and spent many years wandering from town to town, mostly in the south of France. In about 1544 he married a rich widow and settled in the town of Salon, where he seems to have been mainly engaged in the business of manufacturing cosmetics. However, he began to spend more and more of his time in the study of astrology and magic. By 1550 he was fully committed to the business of prophecy, and he issued his first almanac. Almanacs filled with prophecies were popular at the time. Nostradamus soon built a solid reputation as a compiler of almanacs.

His fame, however, rests on the *Centuries,* books of four-line prophetic verses called quatrains. Nearly a thousand of these are arranged in the ten books of the *Centuries*. They were supposed to contain prophecies for the next two thousand years, or specifically until the year 3797. The first edition appeared in 1555, but complete editions were not issued until 1557.

Being a prophet in the sixteenth century could be hazardous to one's health. A prophet might be accused of witchcraft—an offense that carried the death penalty. Luckily for Nostradamus, he had gained the favor of Queen Catherine de Médici, patron of astrologers and magicians.

Ironically, Nostradamus's most famous prophecy concerned the untimely death of Catherine's husband, King Henry II, who was killed in a jousting tournament accident. Many people confused a prophecy with a curse, and Nostradamus was burned in effigy and nearly burned for real, but the queen protected him. He became very famous and wealthy and died July 1, 1566, after predicting his own death.

Since his death, the *Centuries* have been republished, translated and interpreted unceasingly to this day. Many believe they have found predictions of everything from the rise of Napoleon to World War II in this sixteenth-century work.

Unfortunately, the prophecies are not nearly as clear as one might hope. They are couched in vague language and filled with

The magic mirror in which Nostradamus was supposed to have shown
Queen Catherine the future monarchs of France.

obscure symbols. Nostradamus said he deliberately made his
prophecies hard to understand because "rulers, sects and reli-
gions would find them so little to their liking that they could
condemn them. My writings will be better understood by those
who come after my death and by those who penetrate my
meaning."

Often those who interpret Nostradamus find the meaning they
want. During World War I, Frenchmen found a prediction of a
French victory in the *Centuries* while Germans saw clear signs
of a German victory.

Those who interpret Nostradamus are much better at relating
the prophet's words to things that have already happened than
they are at using the quatrains to predict what will happen in
the days and years that follow their interpretation.

Currently, interest in Nostradamus is high, for many believe he has predicted great and terrible events for the end of the millennia in the year 1999. This would appear to fit in with other prophecies of the end of the world before the year 2000. However, since Nostradamus predictions are supposed to run well into the third millennia he clearly could not be predicting the end of the world.

AMELIA EARHART

There may be more myth than mystery in the disappearance of the celebrated pilot Amelia Earhart in 1937. She was one of the most famous women in the world, certainly the most famous woman aviator. She had done just about everything a pilot of the day could, except circle the globe. No other woman had yet circled the globe at any latitude, and Earhart planned to do it at the equator, the longest way round.

For the flight, she had a specially modified Lockheed Electra. Her companion on the flight was Fred Noonan, a fellow adventurer and possibly the best aerial navigator in the world.

By July 2 three-quarters of the journey had been completed with relative ease. But both pilot and navigator were extremely tired, and they faced the most difficult part of the trip, a twenty-four-hour, 2,556-mile flight from Lae in New Guinea to little Howland Island in the middle of the Pacific. The island was just about at the end of the Electra's range, with little room for error. The island is difficult to locate even with today's navigation equipment. While Earhart's equipment was state of the art for the time, and the U.S. Navy had stationed ships all along the proposed route to help provide radio direction, the equipment was primitive by today's standards.

About four hours before the estimated arrival time at Howland Island the Coast Guard cutter *Itasca* began receiving messages from Earhart indicating that she was not sure where she was and that fuel was running low. She did not acknowledge return messages and probably did not receive them. Her own messages were too brief for the *Itasca* to get any fix on her position.

The final message was received at 8:44 A.M., July 3. Within a few hours a huge search was begun. Four thousand men in ten ships and sixty-five airplanes scoured 250,000 square miles of the Pacific over a period of sixteen days. It was the largest search ever made for a single plane. The searchers found nothing.

Over the nearly sixty years since the disappearance, a large number of theories as to what happened have been advanced.

Amelia Earhart and navigator Fred Noonan shortly before they took off on their final flight. (UPI photo)

The most sensational is that the round-the-world flight was a cover, and Earhart and Noonan were really on a spy mission to gather information on Japanese naval installations in the Marshall Islands. According to this theory their plane was shot down by the Japanese, and the pair were either killed or captured. The most elaborate version of the spy theory holds that Earhart and Noonan survived the war in a Japanese prison camp and were secretly brought back to the United States where they took up new lives under assumed names.

There is not a shred of evidence to support this theory, and the woman who was supposed to be the real Amelia Earhart, vehemently, publicly and very credibly, denied it.

The most probable explanation is the obvious one. The plane got lost and went down in the ocean after it ran out of fuel. But the search for Amelia Earhart continues. In 1992 several researchers said they found evidence that Earhart and Noonan had managed to reach a small island after they ditched their plane and survive there at least for a while.

D. B. COOPER

He was so ordinary looking that later, when witnesses tried to describe him, they could come up with absolutely no unusual or distinguishing features. He was wearing a brown business suit and dark glasses and carried a briefcase when he bought a ticket in the Portland, Oregon, airport for Northwest Airlines flight 305, on Thanksgiving eve, 1971. He gave the name Dan

Cooper. A newspaper reporter mistakenly called him D. B. Cooper, and that name stuck.

When the Boeing 727 was in the air, Cooper coolly handed the flight attendant a note saying his briefcase contained a bomb, and if the plane was not to be blown up he was to be given $200,000 in twenty-dollar bills and four parachutes when the plane landed in Seattle.

The airline agreed to the demand, and in Seattle Cooper allowed all of the passengers and most of the crew to depart. He then ordered the plane to take off and fly at a low altitude to Reno, Nevada. The skyjacker was alone in the passenger compartment, and somewhere over the wilderness of the Pacific Northwest he bailed out and became an American folk hero. He has been the subject of books, songs and at least one film.

An exhaustive search for the air pirate was conducted, but no trace of him was ever found. Most investigators doubt that he could have survived the jump, and if he did he would have been injured and not have lived long in the wilderness. It was not too surprising that no body was found. He may have landed in the water or simply lay undiscovered among the trees. The search turned up two bodies of missing men who were not Cooper.

In 1980 an eight-year-old boy found a bundle of twenty-dollar bills washed up on the banks of the Columbia River. These were some of the bills given to the air pirate nine years earlier, but the find did little to clear up the mystery of the fate of D. B. Cooper.

More intriguing than what happened to the skyjacker is the question of who he was. His name certainly was not "Dan Cooper." He must have had some familiarity with aircraft and parachute jumping; perhaps he had once been a paratrooper. He also must have been both bold and desperate, for he would have certainly known how risky it would be to jump from 10,000 feet into the unknown dark below.

While most professional investigators believe "Cooper" died in 1971, some private researchers concluded that he was really Floyd McCoy, a former Green Beret helicopter pilot. McCoy tried an almost identical skyjacking, but he was arrested before

13

Official police artist's sketch of skyjacker D.B. Cooper.

he could jump. Later he escaped and was killed in a shootout with FBI agents. After his arrest McCoy refused to say if he was Cooper.

In another book a woman identified only as Clara said the injured Cooper, then calling himself Paul Cotton, had limped to her isolated home in 1971 and stayed with her until his death from natural causes eleven years later.

Perhaps one day Cooper's remains will be found in the woods, or perhaps an old and sick man, no longer fearing prosecution, will produce the remaining bundles of twenty-dollar bills and prove conclusively that he is the legendary D. B. Cooper.

KASPAR HAUSER

On May 26, 1828, a boy of about seventeen limped into the city of Nuremberg, Germany. He said his name was Kaspar Hauser. But aside from that he seemed to be able to speak only a few words. He would not or could not tell anyone where he came from. He carried no identification but did have two unsigned letters.

The first, dated October 1812, was supposedly written by the boy's mother to someone who was to take care of him. It said Kaspar's father was a soldier but had died. When the boy was seventeen he was to be taken to Nuremberg to join the army. The second letter was from an unnamed "poor laborer" who said that he and his wife had raised the boy in secret and were now sending him to join the army. The "laborer" wrote that he knew nothing of the boy's past. The letters, however, were almost certainly false, for they had both been written by the same person and were quite recent in origin.

At first the boy was thought to be feebleminded, for he just sat and stared at the wall. But he quickly learned to speak and write. He did not, however, shed any light on his past; indeed, his tale deepened the mystery. He said he had lived for as long as he could remember in a dark room, so small that he had been unable even to stand up. He never saw who kept him there. Then one day he was drugged and woke up on the road to Nuremberg.

Rumors circulated that the boy was the illegitimate son of some important person. No one knew who the "important per-

Kaspar Hauser as he first appeared in Nuremberg.

son'' might have been, but candidates were plenty. At first Kaspar received a great deal of attention, which he thoroughly enjoyed. But people soon tired of him. Then one day he was found unconscious with a wound on his head. He alleged that he had been attacked by a mysterious masked man. The attacker was never found, and the wound was not serious.

He was taken to the small town of Ansbach where he again enjoyed temporary fame. On December 14, 1833, Kaspar Hauser, dripping with blood, returned from a walk in the park. He said he had been stabbed by a tall man in a black cloak, and he mumbled something about a purse.

In the park the police found a silk purse with a note inside saying the attacker's name was ''M.L.O.'' but not much else. It had snowed early that day, and at the scene of the alleged attack was only one set of footprints—Kaspar's own.

The wound, which at first seemed to be minor, turned out to be quite serious, and Kaspar died within three days. His final words were ''I didn't do it to myself.''

He was buried under a stone that reads: ''Here lies Kaspar Hauser, Riddle of Our Time. His Birth was Unknown; his Death Mysterious.'' The case has been thoroughly investigated and has been the subject of books, novels, plays and a 1975 film. But the true identity of Kaspar Hauser has never been established.

ALCHEMISTS

Humanity's longest-running and most frustrating quest has been that of the alchemists. Today, alchemists are known primarily for their attempts to turn lead or some other base metal into gold. But that is only part of the story. The true goal of the alchemist was the "philosopher's stone."

Alchemy was based on the philosophy that the universe was unified and harmonious and pervaded by a "universal spirit." This belief could be summed up in the statement, "One is all and all is one." The alchemist's problem was to somehow concentrate and purify matter into a substance that contained the universal spirit in its pristine form. This was the philosopher's stone.

The roots of alchemy stretch back to very ancient times. But Western alchemical theory really became organized in the cosmopolitan city of Alexandria, Egypt, during the first centuries of the Christian era. Alchemy was a combination of magical lore, Greek natural philosophy, Christian doctrine and occasionally a practical knowledge of metalworking.

Hopes, rumors and shared assumptions kept the practice of alchemy alive for many centuries. Though there were stories of alchemists who had distilled the miraculous philosopher's stone, there was certainly no proof. In fact, no one was quite sure what it was supposed to look like. It was often referred to as the elixir or tincture, indicating that it was a liquid and not a stone at all. Whatever it was, it not only had the power to turn base metal into gold, it was said to cure all diseases, prolong life indefinitely and accomplish a whole host of other miraculous things.

Many alchemical texts survive, but it is very difficult to figure out what the alchemists were actually doing, for two reasons. First, alchemy always had a spiritual or mystical side. The belief grew that to be successful the alchemist had to be "spiritually pure." Sometimes it is impossible to determine whether the alchemist is describing a physical experiment or a spiritual exercise. The stress on spiritual purity led to the paradoxical conclusion that to make gold, a man must be pure enough not to want gold.

Second, alchemy is difficult to understand because the alchemists were very suspicious. They deliberately used obscure signs and symbols known only to themselves. Alchemists feared that if they clearly described what they were doing someone might steal their "secret." Most mystical quests are secretive in the belief that the knowledge could be misused by those who are not "pure." And plenty alchemical fakers used a lot of mumbo jumbo to dazzle and distract the unwary.

The result is endless confusion. Sometimes the alchemist abandoned words altogether and used only signs or symbols. Medieval alchemical art is often beautiful and always strange.

The alchemical quest was compelling yet frustrating. Time after time, alchemists reported being just at the point of distilling "the essence" when the retort broke or the crucible cracked, forcing them to start the process all over again.

Alchemy endured for centuries, and it fascinated and even obsessed some of the most brilliant and powerful men of their time. But eventually the whole theory of a universal spirit crumbled in the face of the discoveries of science. By the eighteenth century serious belief in alchemy had all but disappeared. The word itself became almost synonymous with fraud and foolishness.

In defense of alchemy, it can be said that the knowledge gained working with various materials contributed directly to the development of science.

Even today, however, alchemy is not totally dead. A British alchemist named Archibald Cockrin, who died in the 1960s, maintained that he had made a crystal of gold grow like a plant. Occult societies still drop hints that they hold "the secret," and the symbolism of the alchemist is still popular with today's occultists.

NICHOLAS FLAMEL

The alchemists' quest to turn base metals into gold has, according to rumor and legend, succeeded several times. But the strongest case for success is found in the career of a fourteenth-century Frenchman, Nicholas Flamel.

Flamel was a public scribe who wrote letters for people who could not write. He had a flourishing business and married a wealthy wife to whom he was devoted. He had no particular interest in alchemy until he had a strange dream in which he was given a book by an angel. He was told that he would not understand the book at first, but that one day he would see something in it that no one else had seen.

Flamel had almost forgotten the dream when, in 1357, a traveling merchant offered him the very book of which he had dreamed. It was filled with mysterious alchemical symbols and written in a language he could not understand. On the book's first page was a Latin inscription in gold letters saying that the book had been written by Abraham the Jew and that anyone who read it would be cursed "unless he were Sacrificer or Scribe."

Alchemist Nicholas Flamel. Did he discover the secret of making gold?

As a scribe, Flamel felt quite safe from the curse. The Latin inscription went on to say that the text contained the formula used by the Jews to make gold to pay tribute to the Roman Empire. Unfortunately, as the dream foretold, he could make nothing of the rest of the book. The more he studied it the less he understood.

For twenty-one years Flamel tried to crack the book's secret, without success. Finally he decided that since the book had been written for the Jews he would consult Jewish scholars. He met a learned scholar who recognized some copies of drawings from the book that Flamel had made. Though the scholar died before actually seeing the book itself, he gave Flamel enough hints to be able to work out the text.

Flamel recorded that on January 17, 1382, he was able to change half a pound of lead into silver. On April 25 he changed the same amount of lead into gold. He was an extremely cautious man and successfully attempted the transformation only two more times.

He lived quietly, writing about alchemy and doing good works until his death on March 22, 1417. He left behind a notable record of endowments to churches, hospitals and other charitable institutions.

After Flamel's death, neighbors ransacked his property looking for ''the secret.'' They found nothing. Two centuries later people were still digging up the ground, with no greater success.

Supporters of alchemy point to the considerable fortune Flamel amassed as proof that he could make gold.

Stories relate that in addition to finding the secret of making gold, Flamel succeeded in the other great alchemical quest, finding the elixir of life. As a result, he and his wife became immortal. They were reportedly seen alive and well in India in the seventeenth century. In the mid-eighteenth century a number of people testified that the pair had attended the opera in Paris. They have not been heard from recently.

THE LITTLE PEOPLE

Today when you hear the words *fairy tale,* it conjures up images of tiny winged sprites of the Walt Disney Tinkerbell variety. But back in the days when people really believed in fairies, or the little people as they were commonly called, the image was not nearly so benign.

An enormous amount of little people lore can be found all over the world, particularly in northern Europe. In this lore the fairy folk are small in stature, but they are not the tiny creatures of later stories. Sometimes they are very nearly the size of humans. They live secretive lives and are usually indifferent to people. But woe to anyone who ran afoul of them. At one time people were genuinely afraid to wander at night in regions thought to be inhabited by the little people. Anyone who disappeared mysteriously was assumed to have been "taken"—that is kidnapped or killed—by the fairies. Fairies also regularly kidnapped newborn human infants and substituted sickly fairy "changelings" in their place, according to popular belief.

Despite their diminutive stature, the fairies could be lustful creatures, and tales of seduction and rape and even of marriages between humans and the little people are common in folklore. Such marriages traditionally turned out tragically for the human partner.

People who believed in fairies tried to placate them with gifts, usually in the form of food left out at night. Believers attempted to ward fairies off with a variety of magical rituals and spells, that were still used in some isolated rural districts in Britain less than a century ago. As late as the nineteenth century folklorists collected many accounts of what were supposed to be personal encounters with the little people.

By that time, however, belief in the fairy folk had declined. The most interesting firsthand collection of lore was made in the seventeenth century by Reverend Robert Kirk, a Scottish minister, who really believed in fairies. He called them "the Intermediate Unconfirm'd People (betwixt Man and Angell)." One night Reverend Kirk went out for a walk, and the next morning he was found dead on a spot reputed to be used by the little people. There were rumors that he had been "taken" by the fairies because he "knew too much."

A vast number of theories have been proposed to account for fairy lore. Some scholars have seriously proposed that northern Europe was once inhabited by a race of pygmies who fled into the forest before the Celtic invaders arrived. From there they carried on guerrilla warfare until they finally died out or were absorbed by their conquerors. After centuries, goes this theory, memories of real encounters between the Celts and the pygmy race were transformed into semimagical fairy stories.

The theory is extremely attractive, because it ties up all sorts of loose ends. But there is, alas, no material evidence to back it up. The real origin of the myth of the little people remains obscure.

AKHENATON

Between 1375 and 1358 B.C. Egypt was ruled by a very strange and singular man called Akhenaton. He has been called the first monotheist, the first heretic, even the first individualist in history. He has been called an insane egoist whose religious obsession nearly ruined the nation he was supposed to rule.

He was the successor to Amenhotep III, often called "the Magnificent," a king who ruled a vast, prosperous and generally peaceful empire. When he ascended the throne, it was under the name Amenhotep IV, but after a few years he changed his name to Akhenaton. The chief of Egypt's many gods was Amon, whose name was part of the king's original name. Amon was dropped in favor of a new god, Aton. Unlike other Egyptian gods, who were represented in human and animal form, or a combination of the two, Aton was represented only as the disc of the sun with rays, often ending in small hands extending from it.

Whether Aton was thought of as the only god or simply the most powerful is not clear. The king closed the temples of many other gods and was particularly harsh to those of Amon. He tried to have Amon's name removed from documents and temple walls. He moved the capital from Thebes, a city long identified with Amon, to a new city he built in honor of Aton.

Artistic style changed radically. Probably the most famous single piece of Egyptian art, the bust of Akhenaton's wife, Queen Nefertiti, was done in the new style. While Nefertiti is shown as a beauty, the representations of the king himself are grotesque, almost caricatures. For thousands of years Egyptian kings had been shown in stiff, ritualistic settings. Akhenaton's artists portrayed him in domestic scenes, receiving flowers from his queen or playing with his children.

One of the most puzzling questions of the Akhenaton period is this: "Did his religion have any effect on the development of monotheism among the Jews?" Parallels between one of the hymns to Aton, perhaps written by the king himself, and Psalm 104 of the Bible are startling and far too close to be mere coincidence.

All the changes must have been deeply disturbing to the conservative Egyptians and particularly to the powerful priests of Amon. There are also indications that the king was not paying attention to affairs of state, and the empire was crumbling.

Akhenaton's successors moved rapidly to modify and ultimately undo the king's religious revolution. The famous Tutankhamen, who came to the throne just a year or two after Akhenaton's death, had originally been named Tutankaton. The change from Aton back to Amon signified the triumph of the old gods over the new. However, many of the dazzling treasures of Tutankhamen's tomb were made in the realistic style that had developed under Akhenaton. After Tutankhamen, Akhenaton was declared a "criminal," and his name was removed from all inscriptions. Yet a surprising, even an amazing, amount of material from the period survives.

Many mysteries surround Akhenaton. Where did his religion come from? Did he suffer from some sort of illness? Certainly his pictures indicate something was wrong with him.

Finally, what happened to Akhenaton? The tomb he constructed for himself was empty, and nothing indicates it was ever used. Some experts believe a badly preserved mummy found in another tomb is that of the king, but opinions remain divided.

The most intriguing possibility is that upon his death some loyal followers took his mummy and hid it in a secret and yet undiscovered tomb.

THE DEATH OF NAPOLEON

On May 5, 1821, the deposed emperor of France, Napoleon, died in exile on remote Saint Helena Island. An autopsy performed on the body concluded that a growth appeared to be in his stomach. The doctors could not agree on whether the growth was cancerous and if it had been the cause of the emperor's death. Napoleon had been suffering from stomach pains before his death. His own father had died of stomach cancer, and he worried about the disease.

Napoleon also worried about being poisoned and for good reason. After conquering much of Europe, and terrorizing the rulers of all of it, he was finally defeated and sent into exile. He escaped, gathered another army and again threw the ruling families of Europe into a panic. He was defeated again, and in 1815 sent into an even more distant exile.

Even on Saint Helena Napoleon continued to create anxiety in European governments. There were constant rumors of plots to help the former emperor escape. It would have been far more comfortable for the rulers of Europe if their old nemesis was dead. But they couldn't kill him outright; that would create a martyr. Besides, rulers don't like to kill other rulers, even their enemies. It sets a bad precedent. But if Napoleon died from apparently natural causes, that would be just fine.

Napoleon feared, and probably expected, that he would be poisoned. From the moment of his death there were rumors of poisoning. The symptoms he displayed were typical of arsenic poisoning.

Napoleon had originally been buried on Saint Helena, but later, as the political climate of France shifted, he became a hero again. His body was removed and interred in a massive crypt in Paris, from where it is unlikely ever to be exhumed.

However, in the 1960s it was discovered how to detect the presence of arsenic in an individual by testing a single strand of hair. Several locks of Napoleon's hair had been cut as souvenirs on the day after his death, and some were obtained for a test.

The tests showed that Napoleon had received large but not necessarily fatal doses of arsenic during the last months of his life. Arsenic, however, can have a cumulative effect, and repeated doses could have killed him.

The investigators even thought they had found a suspected poisoner. He was Count Charles-Tristan de Montholon, a member of the emperor's staff in exile. They believed that Montholon was in the pay of Napoleon's enemies in France.

However, not a single scrap of documentary evidence supports the conclusion that Napoleon was actually poisoned. Arsenic can enter the human body in many ways without assuming that an unknown poisoner is secretly sprinkling it on the food. In 1982 it was found that Napoleon's wallpaper at Saint Helena contained arsenic.

Short of opening the emperor's tomb and examining his remains, which no one seriously believes will ever be done, the cause of Napoleon's death will remain a mystery.

THE DRUIDS

On the day of the summer solstice, a group of white-robed individuals who call themselves druids, gather at Stonehenge in England to perform what they call an ancient ritual. The annual event usually attracts a large crowd of onlookers and is given a good deal of press attention. It is all a show, for today's druids have nothing to do with the ancient druids. The modern ceremonies are re-creations of what some people believe (without any good evidence) are those the ancient druids performed.

We have little authentic knowledge of the real druids. What we do know comes from the Romans. Since the druids were the priests of the Celtic peoples of Britain and elsewhere, and were enemies of Rome, it is hardly surprising that the picture we have is an unflattering one. The accounts describe terrifying spectacles in which large numbers of people were sacrificed. Since the druids and their religion were wiped out by the Romans they did not have a chance to write their side of the story.

The man who really recreated the druids for modern times was an eccentric eighteenth-century cleric, Dr. William Stukeley. Stukeley first suggested that the druids built Stonehenge. Then he decided that the druids were really the direct descendants of Abraham and the keepers of the pure British religion that was later embodied in the Church of England. Instead of the bloodthirsty savages depicted by the Romans, Stukeley found the druids the noblest of beings, though he did admit that human sacrifice was a failing.

After Stukeley came a flowering of druid societies, some serious, some not so serious. Members paraded about in long white robes, often sporting long, false beards.

Spectators at the druids' Stonehenge ceremonies became so rowdy that they were finally kept away from the ancient monument and only "authentic" druids allowed in. The British government would like to get rid of the druid celebration altogether, but the modern druids have now been around long enough to be considered a recognized religion and have been able to establish a legitimate claim to Stonehenge on the summer solstice.

THE PRINCES IN THE TOWER

Richard III of England has an unparalleled reputation as a monster among British monarchs. He was ruthless in his climb for power and brutal in destroying all who stood in his way. But he was probably no more ruthless and brutal than other kings of his day. However, he had the bad luck to be defeated by Henry Tudor whose descendants ruled England during the lifetime of William Shakespeare, the greatest playwright in history. It was prudent for Shakespeare to vilify enemies of the Tudors, and when he wrote about Richard III, the playwrite turned him into a conniving, murderous, hunchbacked horror, and this may not have been the case. However, Shakespeare depicted Richard III so well that the reputation has stuck.

The most sensational crime attributed to Richard is the murder of his brother and predecessor, Edward IV, and Edward's two children, who were housed, presumably for safekeeping, in the Tower of London. The politics are complicated, but immediately after Edward IV's sudden death in April 1483, his twelve-year-old son became King Edward V. His uncle Richard was made the young man's protector. However, Richard maneuvered to have the young king declared illegitimate, and he became king himself on June 26, 1483.

The Tower of London, in which the young Edward V and his even younger brother were kept, was a grim place. But it was more than a prison, and the two young princes appear to have been housed fairly comfortably at first, but by 1484 they had disappeared. The general opinion at the time and since has been that Richard had the two princes murdered because they were possible rivals, and that the actual killing was done by Richard's henchman, Sir James Tyrrell. Richard always denied this, and no firsthand evidence of the crime was ever presented. On the other hand, Richard was never able to produce the princes themselves or any authentic information on their fate.

Despite Richard III's horrible reputation, or perhaps because of it, he has his passionate defenders. Even today a very active group's aim is to clear the name of the much maligned monarch. Other suspects have been suggested in the killing of the princes, most notably Richard's rival and successor, Henry Tudor, or Henry VII as he became known after he ascended the throne. If the princes had been alive, they would certainly have been a threat to him, too, and Henry was easily as ruthless as Richard. Another suggestion is that the boys died from natural causes. The tower was hardly a healthy environment. The most sensational suggestion is that the boys survived and were concealed in the household of Sir Thomas More. When Henry VII took over, a number of pretenders claimed to be one or another of the royal princes.

Bones allegedly belonging to the two princes were found in the Tower in 1674 and then reburied in Westminster Abbey. They were exhumed and examined in 1933. The conclusion was that they were likely those of the princes and that the boys died in the summer of 1483 shortly after Richard III's coronation. This conclusion has been hotly disputed by Richard's supporters. There is pressure now to exhume the bones again. With modern carbon dating and other techniques it would be possible to learn a great deal more than could be found in 1933.

Even if the bones are conclusively proved to be those of the princes, they will not tell us who murdered the boys or indeed if they were murdered. Richard III remains the most likely suspect. He had both motive and opportunity. But the controversy and the mystery are sure to remain.

SAINT-GERMAIN

The man who called himself the Comte de Saint-Germain must have been a charmer.

He first enters the historical record in about 1740 when he was arrested in London for being a spy. Later he turned up in Germany selling his elixir of life. By 1748 he was in Paris where he became a popular figure at gatherings of the rich and wellborn. Many stories were told of him. This is one:

At a dinner party, Saint-Germain was speaking with easy familiarity of King Richard the Lion-Hearted and of some conversations they had while they were together in the Crusades. When some other guests were openly skeptical, Saint-Germain turned to his valet, who was standing behind his chair, and asked him to confirm the truth of the story.

"I really cannot say, sir," the servant replied. "You forget, sir, I have only been five hundred years in your service."

"Ah! True," said Saint-Germain. "I remember now—it was a little before your time."

But often he made gentle fun of the tales of his extraordinarily long life. When he was told that a Countess de Gergy knew him in Vienna fifty years earlier, and that he looked exactly the same today, Saint-Germain replied:

"That is not impossible, but it is much more possible that the good lady is in her dotage."

He had a reputation for great wealth and often showed off a large collection of jewels, which may have been a mixture of fakes and the real thing. No one knows how he made his money; though he almost certainly worked as a spy, he also lived off the generosity of his many wealthy friends.

He left Paris for unknown reasons in about 1760. From that time, accounts of his comings and goings are vague. He seems to have spent his final days at the court of his friend, the Prince of Hesse-Kassel, dying there in 1782.

What was the Comte de Saint-Germain? Many believe he was nothing more than an extremely clever and charming fraud. Even occultists who revere his memory admit there was much of the actor about him. Yet his life is so shrouded in mystery that there is still room for doubt. His true identity remains unknown. The date and place of his birth are completely unknown, and the time and place of his death are uncertain. There are those who claimed and still claim that Saint-Germain never died. From time to time during the past two centuries people have turned up claiming they had met Saint-Germain or they actually were Saint-Germain. Most commonly it has been said that Saint-Germain has entered that vague realm of the semidivine and immortal masters or adepts.

CAGLIOSTRO

The man who called himself the Count Alessandro de Cagliostro has been described by some as "one of the greatest occult figures of all time" and called by others "the archquack of his age."

Most people believe that Cagliostro was really a Sicilian criminal named Giuseppe Balsamo, born in Palermo around 1743. By 1768 he had married Lorenza Feliciani, the intelligent and beautiful daughter of a bankrupt noble family. The couple, now using the titles the Count and Countess Cagliostro, began traveling throughout Europe telling fortunes, selling alchemical secrets, raising spirits and generally doing whatever itinerant magicians had to do to get along. In London Cagliostro claimed that he knew the secret to picking winning lottery tickets.

It was in France that Cagliostro became most famous or notorious. He said that he had learned the secrets of "Egyptian Freemasonry" from a "curious manuscript" he had come across. He started a secret society and promised that all who became his disciples would be restored to the state of perpetual youth, beauty and innocence that mankind had been deprived of by original sin. His formula for eternal life was a curious mixture of magical theory and the medical practice of the eighteenth century.

Cagliostro became a favorite with the aristocracy of Paris. Somehow he was swept up in a plot to steal a diamond necklace that was supposed to be purchased by Queen Marie Antoinette.

Cagliostro and his wife spent months in the Bastille before ever coming to trial.

Cagliostro defended himself vigorously, giving a colorful account of his own life. The court probably didn't believe what he said, but no real evidence could be presented against him either. He and his wife were acquitted but banished from France. As he fled to England, Cagliostro is supposed to have angrily predicted the French Revolution and the doom of all those who had persecuted him. He was urged by his friends to warn the king and queen, but Cagliostro replied that they would not believe him, and besides, there was no way to change what was predestined.

In 1791 Cagliostro moved to Rome where he tried to start a lodge of his Egyptian Freemasons. It turned out to be a fatal mistake. He was arrested as a heretic and sorcerer and condemned to death. Lorenza was also arrested but was allowed to live on the condition that she "confess" and enter a convent. Ultimately, Cagliostro's death sentence was commuted to life imprisonment. After he tried to escape he was moved to the fortress of San Leo, where he was placed in a tiny dungeon in which he died in 1795.

There are, however, those who claim he did not die in prison but had escaped successfully. Others said that as possessor of the secret of eternal life he could not die. In some occult groups Cagliostro is revered as one of the immortal, semidivine adepts or masters.

At least one twentieth-century biographer has claimed that Cagliostro was not the criminal Balsamo but just who he said he was. Whoever he was (or is), Cagliostro remains a figure of interest in the occult world.

LIZZIE BORDEN

Lizzie Borden took an axe
And gave her mother forty whacks.
When she saw what she had done
She gave her father forty-one.

On a stifling hot day in August 1892, in the small industrial city of Fall River, Massachusetts, someone hacked to death Andrew Jackson Bordon, an elderly and successful businessman in his seventies, and his sixty–four-year-old wife, Abby.

The obvious suspect was their thirty-two-year-old daughter, Lizzie. She had often quarreled with Abby, her father's second wife, and had been heard to complain of her father's miserly ways. She stood to profit handsomely from their deaths. But most significantly, only she and the family servant, Bridget Sullivan, were in the house at the time of the killings. The servant had absolutely no motive for killing the elder Bordons. Besides, if Lizzie was where she said during the murders it would have been impossible for Bridget or almost anyone else to have committed the crime without Lizzie knowing it. Yet she claimed that she saw and heard nothing.

Lizzie Bordon was indicted and in June 1893 brought to trial. The case attracted an enormous amount of attention. All of New England, particularly all of Fall River, was divided into pro- and anti-Lizzie factions.

Andrew Jackson Borden was found hacked to death. (Photo courtesy
of the Fall River Historical Society)

It would seem that the evidence against Lizzie was compelling, even overwhelming; yet the jury deliberated less than an
hour before bringing in a verdict of "not guilty." Later, jury
members reported that they stayed out that long only so they
would not give the appearance of having made a hasty
judgment.

The prosecution case had two major shortcomings. First, the
alleged murder weapon had no bloodstains on it, and second,
Lizzie's clothes had no bloodstains. Of course she could have
washed the axe and burned her clothes. Indeed, evidence
showed that she had burned some clothes after the crime. It
seems that jury members just refused to believe that an otherwise respectable, church-going, middle-aged woman could have
committed such a horrid crime.

Lizzie continued to live quite respectably in Fall River,
though she moved to a more elegant and spacious house. When
she died in 1927 she left an estate of more than two hundred

thousand dollars, some thirty thousand of which she bequeathed to a society for the prevention of cruelty to animals.

To her dying day Lizzie continued to proclaim her innocence, though the general perception grew that she was indeed guilty. Lizzie has also had her persistent and passionate defenders. Over the years a stream of books and articles has been produced trying to prove that someone else wielded the axe. Every bit of evidence in this celebrated case has been examined and reexamined.

While the case against Lizzie remains persuasive, there is also a nagging doubt, and there probably always will be.

ANASTASIA

On the night of July 16, 1918, Tsar Nicholas II of Russia and his family, along with a few of the Imperial family's loyal servants, were herded into a basement room in a house in the mining town of Ekaterinburg where they had been held prisoner, and shot. The bodies were then reputedly taken to a disused mine and burned; any bones remaining were dissolved with acid, and the ashes were thrown down the mineshaft.

The tsar had been deposed and arrested by the Bolsheviks, but Russia was still in the grip of a vicious civil war with the outcome very much in doubt. A living tsar or any member of the Imperial family might serve as a focus for resistance to the revolution. Even identifiable remains might become inspiring relics to the enemies of the Bolsheviks.

The basic facts surrounding the execution of the Imperial

family are not in doubt. Yet without a body or some other physical proof of death it was always possible for someone to turn up claiming that he or she was a member of that family. Such things had happened before, particularly in Russian history. Before long a series of individuals proclaiming to be members of the Imperial Romanov family who had somehow escaped execution came forward. Of all the members of the Imperial family, the one whose identity was claimed most often was the tsar's youngest daughter, Anastasia. There were some fifteen claimants, but only one whose claim has ever been taken seriously.

This claimant turned up in a Berlin hospital in 1920 after she had tried to drown herself. She was about twenty years old, carried no papers or other identification and would not tell anyone who she was. Someone at the hospital read an article about the tsar and his family and was struck by the resemblance between the unknown woman and a picture of Anastasia. At first the woman herself did not claim that she was the tsar's daughter, but by the autumn of 1921 she declared that she was indeed Her Imperial Highness the Grand Dutchess Anastasia Nicholaivna. Thus began a long and inconclusive saga of claim and counterclaim.

The woman said she had not been shot along with the rest of the Imperial family but had fainted and then was smuggled out of Russia by a family with secret tsarist sympathies. She said she had been abandoned by her protectors in Berlin, and that is why she had tried to kill herself.

Some members of the Russian emigré community said they recognized her as the tsar's daughter, while others denounced her as a fraud. She ultimately moved to the United States where she began a legal battle to inherit the tsar's property. The case was to become the longest lawsuit in history. It was not settled until 1970, when the West German Supreme Court dismissed the woman's final appeal.

After World War II the woman moved back to Europe and again became world news as the result of a popular book, a film and many magazine articles. She returned to America to marry a professor of history and died in 1984 at the age of eighty-three, still insisting that she was the tsar's daughter.

However, a good deal of evidence indicates that the woman who called herself Anastasia was really a Polish peasant girl, one of the hundreds of thousands of displaced persons in Europe after World War I.

Since the collapse of Communism in Russia, more evidence about the fate of the Imperial family has been revealed. There is even the possibility that the remains were not fully destroyed, and the bones of the Romanovs, Anastasia's among them, have been located. If this turns out to be true, the mystery of Anastasia will have finally been solved.

THE MURDER OF SIR EDMUND

In 1678, religious feelings ran high in England. There were rumors that the Roman Catholic Church was attempting to recapture the influence it had lost when Henry VIII broke with Rome. The reigning monarch, Charles II, had Catholic sympathies, but he really didn't care much about religion one way or the other.

Stirring the pot of religious hatred was a despicable character by the name of Titus Oates. He was a professional informer and lifelong liar who had concocted a tale of a vast Catholic conspiracy to murder Charles II and place his staunchly Catholic brother James on the throne. The affair became known as the "Popish Plot."

Oates and his associates brought their bogus information to

Sir Edmund Berry Godfrey, a respected magistrate. Whether Godfrey actually put any stock in Oates's tale is unclear. Though he said he felt threatened, he never took any special precautions for his own safety.

On the night of October 12, 1678, the magistrate left his home in London and disappeared. Five days later, his corpse was discovered in a ditch on Primrose Hill, Hampstead. He had been beaten, strangled and run through with a sword—twice. The murderer was taking no chances.

Oates and his associates insisted that the magistrate had been murdered by Catholics because of his part in the investigation. Two months later a man named Miles Prance confessed, under torture, that he had been present when Godfrey was murdered in the courtyard of the home of a wealthy Catholic. Three Catholic servants were named as the murderers.

Given the overheated atmosphere of the time, the fate of the three men was sealed as soon as the accusation was made, though Oates and his associates failed in their attempts to have more prominent people convicted for the crime. Still, the murder did much to fan the flames of the Popish Plot hysteria.

Who did kill Sir Edmund Godfrey? Almost certainly not the three men who were beheaded for the crime. Suggestions have been made that the murder was inspired by Oates or more powerful anti-Catholics to whip up public feeling. Or that the murder may have been committed by the Earl of Pembroke, a drunken and violent nobleman who had a personal grudge against the magistrate. He had been convicted of manslaughter before Magistrate Godfrey for stomping a man to death.

This murder, which had such far-reaching consequences, remains unsolved.

THE UNKNOWN HOAXER

The Piltdown Man was the greatest scientific fraud of the century—perhaps the greatest scientific fraud of all times.

Beginning in 1908 Charles Dawson, an amateur geologist and archaeologist, began finding what appeared to be fragments of a very ancient human skull in a gravel pit at Piltdown Common near a small village in Sussex, England. By 1912 enough material had been found to be able to reconstruct the entire skull. The top of the skull had a large and remarkably modern brain case while the jaw was heavy and apelike. It looked like the perfect "missing link" between apes and humans, and it indicated that the human brain had developed early in evolutionary history.

At the time the Piltdown discoveries were made, not a great deal of human fossil material was available to compare it with. But as the years passed and more discoveries were made, Piltdown Man no longer seemed to fit in, for it became clear that the large brain was a late evolutionary development.

Mistakes are often made in identifying fossils, but Piltdown Man was no mistake, and by the early 1950s scientists had begun to think the unthinkable, that the fossil was an elaborate fake. A close examination of the bones showed that the skull fragments were those of a modern man stained to resemble a fossil and that the jawbone was that of an orangutan, in which the teeth had been ground down to resemble human shape. All of the other fossil material found in the gravel pit had either been faked or were real fossils that had been planted there. The whole thing had been an elaborate and remarkably successful hoax that had bamboozled the scientific world for over three decades.

But who was the faker?

The obvious suspect is Dawson himself. The discovery made him world famous. While the hoax probably could not have been carried out without Dawson's aid, most investigators doubt that he had the knowledge or technical skill to do it alone.

There has been no shortage of other suspects. Probably the wildest is Sir Arthur Conan Doyle, creator of Sherlock Holmes. Doyle didn't live far from where the Piltdown discoveries were made. He had been trained as a physician, but by the time of Piltdown he had become a convinced spiritualist, a belief ridiculed by most scientists. It has been suggested that Doyle cooked up the hoax to put one over on orthodox science. However, there is no credible evidence that the painfully honest Doyle would, or even could, have carried off such a fraud.

More likely suspects can be found among the scientists connected with the Piltdown discovery. Pierre Teilhard de Chardin, a young French priest who was to go on to a distinguished career in paleontology, has been implicated. Teilhard was a friend of Dawson's and was on the scene early. It has been speculated that for him it was a youthful prank that just got out of hand.

More recently, fingers have been pointed at Sir Arthur Keith, an anatomist and museum conservator who was the first to trumpet the great significance of the find. According to this theory it was no prank, but a deliberate attempt to alter the course of paleontology.

But no one has left behind a confession, and no "smoking gun" evidence has been found. There will probably always be controversy over the question of who pulled this one off.

JACK THE RIPPER

No other killer in history has attained the legendary status of the serial killer known as Jack the Ripper. There have been killers who have had more victims and have been more prominent. The Ripper had only five confirmed victims, and they were prostitutes of the lowest class, whose deaths under more ordinary circumstances would have gone virtually unnoticed. The killings were gruesome, but there have been worse. The Ripper was never caught, but there are lots of unsolved murders.

His fame is due in part to the time and place of the murders—1888, the height of the Victorian era in fog-shrouded, gas-lit London. It is the London of Sherlock Holmes, Dr. Jekyll and Mr. Hyde. Even Dracula is said to have visited London in 1887. Then there is the killer's catchy name, which the murderer himself may have signed to some taunting letters sent to the police (though it is possible that the letters were a newspaperman's hoax). Finally there is the sheer audacity of the crimes, one of which was committed nearly under the noses of the police.

The Ripper's first known crime took place on the night of August 31, 1888, in the seedy Whitechapel district of London. The victim was forty-two-year-old Mary Ann Nicholls. The murderer first cut her throat, then slit her abdomen open.

A week later the victim was forty-seven-year-old Annie Chapman. The circumstances were almost identical to those in the first killing.

It was this second killing that made the police and public

take notice. Whitechapel was flooded with uniformed police, and businessmen from the district formed a committee that hired private detectives and organized civilian volunteers to patrol the area.

Despite all the precautions, on September 29 the Ripper committed not one murder but two. A witness discovered the body of a woman whose throat had just been cut. The blood was still pouring from the wound. He actually heard footsteps, undoubtedly those of the murderer in the darkness. Jack the Ripper had been interrupted at his work before he had time to perform the usual mutilations. Within an hour he had killed and mutilated a second victim. He had done so with such skill, or luck, that a watchman sitting just a few yards away never saw or heard a thing.

These were extremely bloody crimes, and the murderer must have been covered with blood. Yet somehow he escaped through streets swarming with constables and volunteer vigilantes without being noticed.

The final victim, Mary Kelly, was killed six weeks later. This was the only Ripper crime that took place indoors. In comparative privacy the killer had several hours in which to butcher his victim completely. The scene the police found on the morning of November 10, 1888, was literally indescribable.

That was the final Ripper murder. Within a month of Mary Kelly's murder the extra police were withdrawn and the citizens' committee disbanded. Privately, committee members were told by police that the Ripper had killed himself. The man suspected was Montague John Druitt, a failed lawyer who had drowned himself on December 3, 1888. He left a suicide note, but its contents have never been made public.

Plenty of other suspects have ranged from a mad Russian immigrant doctor named Michael Ostrog to the Duke of Clarence, Queen Victoria's grandson who would have become king if he had not died young. Some also speculated that the killings were carried out by a cabal of Freemasons or that the killer was a woman. A recently published "diary," which is supposed to prove the Ripper was one James Maybrick, who may have

The Ripper murders, as covered in the newspapers of the time.

been murdered by his wife at about the time the Ripper killings ended, is almost certainly a hoax.

All surviving records of the case now appear to have been made public. There is some reason to believe that records were lost or destroyed over the years, but it is probable that now we know all we ever will about Jack the Ripper.

WHAT HAPPENED TO HOFFA?

No one doubts that Jimmy Hoffa was murdered. It is not one of those missing persons cases where the subject is rumored to have run off to a tropical island or a monastery in Tibet.

Hoffa had been head of the powerful Teamster's Union, and he owed part of his power to his close alliance with organized-crime figures. In 1967 he was convicted of a number of offenses but continued to control the union from prison. He was finally given a conditional release by President Richard Nixon in 1971 in return for union support in the election. However, one provision of the release was that Hoffa could not hold any union office. This was not a prohibition that Hoffa was very happy with and he began a campaign to have the prohibition lifted. But by this time the new leaders of the union had made their own deals with the mob.

On July 30, 1975, Hoffa went to a Detroit restaurant where he thought he was going to meet some powerful organized-crime figures and line up their support. They never showed. Hoffa was seen driving away from the restaurant with a couple other men, and he was never seen again.

Former Teamsters Union President Jimmy Hoffa disappeared without a trace. (Wide World photo)

Since that time investigators have dragged rivers and lakes, dug up fields and drilled through concrete floors in an attempt to find the Teamster leader's remains. The searches have always been unsuccessful.

Rumors have suggested that his body was sunk in a swamp, put in a car crusher, dissolved in a vat of chemicals or even dumped in the concrete used to build the New Jersey Giants' football stadium.

In fact, no one knows exactly what happened to Jimmy Hoffa, or to be more exact, someone knows, but no one is telling.

ROBIN HOOD

The British treat the two great legendary figures of their history very differently. King Arthur, if he existed at all, lived in the sixth century. Yet *Debrett's Peerage,* the book that officially chronicles the family histories of the aristocracy, not only accepts the reality of Arthur, but tries to tie him directly to the present monarch.

Robin Hood lived much later, probably the thirteenth century, a time when records were more accurate. The tales of Robin are nowhere near as fantastic as those that have grown up around Arthur. Yet Robin Hood is routinely dismissed as a fictional character.

The difference in attitude has as much to do with social class as with history. Arthur was a king, and Robin was a robber. He was a well-mannered, well-meaning robber, a man who stole mainly from greedy monks. He was no rebel. But, when all was said and done, he was still a robber and a fairly lowborn one at that.

Historians have attempted to identify Robin as Robert Earl of Huntington, who had been done some sort of injustice and was forced to flee into the forest to take up the life of an outlaw. Unfortunately, no Robert Earl of Huntington ever existed. All the early stories and ballads about Robin show very clearly that Robin was a simple yeoman, nothing more.

Historian J. C. Holt studied the legend and found a bewilderingly large number of candidates for the real Robin Hood. One candidate is Robert Hode, who fled from the law at York (just north of Sherwood Forest) in 1225. Another may be part of an entire family named Hood who lived in the area in the thirteenth century. The family either brought forth the original Robin Hood or adopted the Robin Hood traditions. There was even a family with the surname Robynhod. Holt concludes, "It is more likely than not that ... the original of the story was a real person."

As the story developed, details from popular romances about other real-life outlaws and purely fictional elements were added.

THE VANISHING EARL

Britain's most aristocratic missing person is Richard John Bingham, the seventh earl of Lucian. He had been dubbed Lucky Lucian by the press, though his life seemed to belie that title.

He had spent much of his life throwing away the family fortune over the gambling tables. His marriage went disastrously wrong and ended in a bitter and expensive custody fight that Lucian lost.

Lucian became depressed and began drinking even more heavily. He was obsessed with his children and his hatred for his wife, who he believed was trying to turn the children against him. He had even begun hanging around the fashionable Belgravia home that his wife, Veronica, had won in the settlement.

On the night of November 7, 1974, Veronica, bloody and hysterical, rushed into a Belgravia pub, shouting, "He's murdered the nanny! The children are in the house! He's in the house!''

The police found the battered body of Sandra Rivett, a newly hired nanny, but the children were unharmed.

Later that same night, Lord Lucian, drunk and disheveled, went to the home of some friends in Sussex. He told them a wild story about seeing someone break into the house in Belgravia. After letting himself in with his own key, he said, he found the intruder struggling with a woman he believed to be Veronica. He rushed to save her but slipped in a pool of blood, and the intruder got away. He also said that he was sure his wife would blame him for what had happened and that he would have to ''lie doggo for a while.''

The story sounds unbelievable, and that's what the police thought when Lucian's friends finally told them. Lucian had

Is "Lucky" Lord Lucian still hiding out somewhere?

stayed at his friend's house until about one A.M., and after he left was never seen again. His friends did not bother to inform police of the extraordinary events until later the following day.

Police were to encounter that pattern throughout the investigation. No one in what came to be called the "Lucian set" was particularly helpful in the search for the missing earl.

On November 10 the car Lucian had been driving that night was found in the port city of Newhaven. The interior was blood-stained, and a length of lead pipe wrapped in tape was found in the trunk. The assumption is that Lucian, realizing that he faced trial and almost certain conviction, drowned himself. But no body has ever been found, and as many suspect that he is still alive and in hiding. Lady Lucian has never asked that her husband be declared legally dead.

Serious questions about this case remain unanswered.

LORD GORDON-GORDON

One of the greatest con men in history was a tall aristocratic-looking fellow who called himself (among other names) Lord Gordon-Gordon. He showed up in Minneapolis in 1871 claiming to be a fabulously wealthy Scottish nobleman who was going to buy vast tracts of land on which to settle Scottish immigrants. He was treated like royalty for months.

He then made his way to New York City where he impressed Horace Greeley, the powerful editor of the *New York Tribune,* with the story that he was about to buy control of the Erie Railroad, which was then owned by the notorious robber baron

Jay Gould. Greeley spread the word that Gould was going to be kicked out, and the old robber baron panicked. Gould promised Gordon-Gordon that he would reform and gave him a million dollars in cash and stocks as a pledge of his good will. Getting money out of Gould, without even giving him a written receipt, was an astonishing feat, for Gould himself had spent his life cheating everyone else.

However, Gordon-Gordon's plot began to unravel, and Gould demanded his money back. He got it, minus $150,000. Gould took Gordon-Gordon to court where the Englishman appeared utterly confident and supplied names of prominent people in England who he said would verify his claims. By this time Gould's agents were scouring England, and they discovered that there was no Lord Gordon-Gordon. In fact, some years earlier this same man, calling himself Lord Glencarin, had swindled an Edinburgh jeweler out of $25,000.

With his scheme collapsing around him, the bogus nobleman took the night train to Canada. He charmed the people of Fort Gerry, Canada, and was able to hold off Gould, the Edinburgh jeweler and the people of Minneapolis—at least for a while. Finally, though, the Canadian government agreed to extradite him.

In 1873 he gave a grand going-away party for the people of Fort Gerry. As he was arrested, he excused himself, saying he needed time to pack. He went into another room and calmly blew his brains out.

The money that Lord Gordon-Gordon stole was never found. He never revealed his true identity, and no one has ever been able to discover who he really was.

IN A MAN'S WORLD

For nearly fifty years Billy Tipton was one of the most well-regarded figures in American jazz. The saxophonist and pianist had played with the big bands back in the 1930s and '40s. After the big-band era ended he formed his own Billy Tipton Trio and continued to play smaller clubs, almost up to the time of his death in 1989.

Tipton was an affable fellow, well liked by his fellow musicians. And for a jazz musician he appeared to lead an exceptionally stable and conventional life. He had been married and divorced once. During his marriage he had adopted three sons who had thought of him as an exemplary father. He was also a scoutmaster and general all-around good citizen.

When he died of a bleeding ulcer, his passing was mourned by all who knew him. But as it turned out, nobody really knew him. When physicians examined the body after the jazzman's death, they found out that he was really a woman.

None of Tipton's friends, neighbors or fellow musicians had ever suspected anything of the sort. His three sons were shocked. Even his ex-wife, Kitty, maintained she never knew. She said that Tipton had told her that he had suffered a severe injury that had sexually incapacitated him.

Those who know the jazz scene assume that Tipton took on a male identity because instrumental jazz was completely closed to women, no matter how talented.

What is astonishing is that Tipton was able to carry on the deception so long, while living a very public life. And to this day Billy Tipton's original identity has never been revealed; it may be a secret Tipton carried to the grave.

MOUND BUILDERS

Mounds, some colossal in size or constructed in the shape of snakes, bears or other animals, dot the American Midwest. For a long time learned men in America attributed these mounds to Greeks, Persians, Romans, Vikings, Hindus, Phoenicians, the Ten Lost Tribes of Israel or any other Old World civilization that built, or was believed to have built, any sort of mound. The mounds were also attributed to migrants from South America or China or to refugees from the sinking of Atlantis.

When the mounds were excavated they were often found to be burial mounds containing bones and a small number of simple tools, weapons and pottery. They contained no evidence whatever of Hebrew or Atlantean origin or evidence that would connect them with any other advanced civilization, real or imagined. Yet the belief in the vanished race of mound builders flourished.

Why a vanished race? In their new world the European settlers of North America found no great monuments like the pyramids of Egypt or South America. All they found were the mounds, and they wanted to connect them somehow with the great civilizations of antiquity and perhaps with people and events mentioned in the Bible.

The obvious mound builders were the ancestors of the American Indians who inhabited the areas in which the mounds were found. The Indians said their ancestors had built the mounds, and some of the tribes were still actively engaged in mound building. But that conclusion was not as romantic and satisfying as conjuring up an unknown race of mound builders. Besides, the Indians were regarded as primitive savages with whom the white man was contesting for land. It was embarrassing to admit that the Indians could have built anything more permanent than a wigwam.

The myth of a vanished race of mound builders served another purpose. If the mound builders were not Indians, then they had been exterminated by the Indians. Thus, when the settlers drove the Indians off the land, they were in a sense only taking back what the savages had already stolen from others, perhaps even from the white man's own ancestors.

Finally, a series of careful investigations proved beyond any doubt, reasonable or unreasonable, that the mounds were not built by a lost race, but by the ancestors of the Indians.

While the myth of the lost race of mound builders is quite dead today, it is useful to recall just how vigorously it once flourished and why.

JUDGE CRATER

On the night of August 6, 1930, Joseph Force Crater, a justice of the New York Supreme Court, stepped into a taxi on Forty-fifth Street in New York City and was never heard from again. He became, far and away, the most famous missing man in America.

Judge Crater was an important man. He was regarded as having one of the best legal minds in the country and had just been appointed to the highest court in New York. There was talk that he might ultimately go to the U.S. Supreme Court.

He was spending the summer with his wife, Stella, at their vacation home in Maine. On August 2 he received a mysterious phone call. "I've got to straighten those fellows out," he told Stella. The next morning he took the train to New York.

In New York he went directly to his Fifth Avenue apartment, told the maid he would be staying only a few days and then suggested she take those days off. He spent the next day in his office tending to legal business. The following day, the sixth, Judge Crater was back in his office. He had his assistant cash two checks totaling $51,000, and said, "Get large bills." He shoved the cash in his pocket without even counting it.

He also bundled up a large quantity of papers from his office files and took them home. No trace of the missing files was ever found.

That evening he bought a ticket to a popular Broadway show. The judge met a show-business lawyer he knew and his chorus girlfriend and joined them for dinner. At 9:15, after a leisurely dinner, he hailed a taxi to go to the theater, though he could easily have walked the short distance, and he was already late for the first act.

After a few days without word from her husband, Stella began to worry. She sent the family chauffeur to New York to find out when he was coming back. Next she called some of the judge's friends who assured her that he would soon reappear. But he didn't.

Still it was a full month after Crater disappeared before it was officially reported to the police and an investigation began.

Judge Crater was not nearly as respectable a fellow as he appeared. He had close ties with the corrupt Tammany Hall machine that ran New York City politics. A serious investigation of corruption had begun, and while no charges were ever leveled against Crater, many of his cronies were in trouble. He was a womanizer who had a long-time mistress, and he had

Judge Joseph Crater was once the most famous missing person in America.

lots of affairs on the side. He was also a regular patron of nightclubs owned and frequented by New York's most notorious gangsters.

The investigation turned up no evidence of illegal activity on Crater's part, certainly nothing that would make him want to disappear. But there is good reason to believe that the investigation was not as thorough as it might have been. Even his wife was remarkably unhelpful.

In the years that followed, Crater was "sighted" everywhere from a monastery in Mexico to a gambling house in East Africa. He was rumored to have run away, been murdered or died of a heart attack. Detectives, reporters, even psychics have offered their explanations, all different. Not a scrap of authentic new evidence has turned up since 1930, and in the files of the New York City police, the case remains officially open.

THE MISSING MARINER

When the trimaran (a three-hulled yacht) *Teignmouth Electron* was found floating abandoned in the Atlantic Ocean some 700 miles southwest of the Azores on July 10, 1969, it presented two mysteries. First, what had happened to its skipper, Donald Crowhurst? Crowhurst was an experienced sailor, and the trimaran was in good order—there was no obvious reason why it should have been abandoned. The second mystery was why the boat, which was supposed to be leading in a round-the-world solo sailing race, was nowhere near where it should have been.

An examination of Crowhurst's logbooks revealed a bizarre

story. Crowhurst's voyage had been underfinanced and badly planned. He almost immediately began having problems, and it became obvious, probably within days, that he would never be able to successfully complete the 30,000-mile voyage. Instead of simply admitting defeat he began radioing reports of splendid progress to his press agent. He also kept a false log of his success. A second and true log showed a sailor near despair. He made a clandestine and, in terms of the rules of the race, illegal stop for repairs at a remote port in South America. Though he ultimately covered 17,000 miles, he never actually got out of the Atlantic.

Apparently, he planned to return home to England, somewhere back in the pack of the racers, and be hailed as a gallant loser. In that position his reports would probably never have been closely examined. In an ironic twist of fate, virtually all the other competitors had, for one reason or another, dropped out of the race—and Crowhurst looked like a sure winner. In the glare of publicity, his fraud would not have held up for a moment.

The entries in his journal became more and more bizarre, ending with "I will resign the game . . . There is no reason for harmful . . ."

Some cynics maintain that Crowhurst faked the mental confusion that appeared in his journal and that he really went ashore somewhere and is still in hiding. Others say that Crowhurst, who had the reputation of being clumsy, fell overboard. Most believe that by "resigning the game" Crowhurst meant that he deliberately jumped overboard and drowned. We will probably never know.

DOROTHY ARNOLD

On December 12, 1910, twenty-five-year-old Dorothy Arnold left her parents' luxurious Manhattan apartment for a shopping trip down Fifth Avenue. Early in the afternoon she met a friend, chatted for a few moments, waved good-bye and was never seen again.

The disappearance of the daughter of one of New York's wealthiest and most prominent families would have created a sensation at any time, but her family's reaction made it doubly odd. At first they contacted friends and private detectives but did not report the disappearance to the police for six weeks.

Her father, seventy-three-year-old Francis Arnold, wanted to keep the whole thing out of the newspapers. The police told him publicity would be useful in locating his daughter; besides, the press already had hints of the story. When Arnold met with reporters he said his daughter had probably been murdered and her body thrown into the Central Park reservoir. When asked about possible boyfriends, the old man exploded and stormed out.

It didn't take reporters long to locate a boyfriend, though he was no boy. He was George Griscom, Jr.—he was forty-two years old, but everyone still called him Junior. Dorothy and Junior had spent a week together in Boston, which was quite a scandalous thing to do in 1910. However, Junior was out of the country when Dorothy disappeared; besides, he had no reason to kill her and was not the murdering sort.

Dorothy had wanted to be a writer, but her parents had ridiculed her ambition. When one of her stories was turned down by a magazine, she was deeply depressed and wrote a letter to a friend containing these ominous words: "Mother will always think an accident has happened." That was just a few weeks before she disappeared.

The most probable explanation is that a depressed Dorothy had committed suicide, perhaps by jumping from one of the numerous New York ferryboats. It is also probable that her family knew or strongly suspected what had happened and tried to cover it up. Suicide was considered a grave sin, and it would have embarrassed the entire family. Murder, kidnapping or just plain running away are also possible but less likely explanations. A police inspector who worked on the case hinted that the Arnold family had always known what had happened, but later he recanted that statement.

Then there is the poetic explanation offered by one contemporary. He noted that the day after Dorothy disappeared a beautiful white swan appeared in the Central Park lagoon. The unhappy girl, he said, had been changed into a swan.

SHAKESPEARE

William Shakespeare is generally regarded as the greatest dramatist ever to write in English—or any other language. Yet for several centuries there has been a small but amazingly persistent group that has insisted that the plays attributed to William Shakespeare were not written by him.

There are two basic reasons for the anti-Shakespeare theories. First, for a man who has become so famous we have astonishingly little authentic information about his life. William Shakespeare was born in the village of Stratford-upon-Avon on April 26, 1564. His father appears to have been a reasonably prosperous and possibly illiterate butcher who later lost most of his fortune. There is no record that William ever went to school, though he probably received some sort of education. He married Anne Hathaway sometime around 1582, and the couple had three children. In 1592 Shakespeare was in London where he was beginning to build a modest reputation as an actor and playwright. There are scattered references to his life in London. By 1613 he had apparently earned enough money to retire to Stratford where he never wrote another word, except perhaps a bit of doggeral and distinctly un-Shakespearean verse that appears on his gravestone. He died in 1616 in relative obscurity. Shakespeare's real fame was not to come until years after his death.

The second reason that anti-Shakespeare theories flourish is the conviction that this low born, poorly educated *actor* could not possibly have written the plays and poems attributed to him. In those days acting was not considered a respectable profession. William Shakespeare's will indicates that he did not possess a single copy of any of his plays or indeed any other book. Shakespeare, say the anti-Shakespeareans, was simply a front man, hired to put his name on the words of a greater and nobler mind.

Chief candidate for the man behind Shakespeare's works is Sir Francis Bacon, sometime friend of Queen Elizabeth and one of the most brilliant men of his time. Speculation about Bacon having written the plays of Shakespeare began as early as 1785. The most enthusiastic, indeed obsessed, proponent of the theory was an American schoolteacher and lecturer named Della Bacon (no relation to Sir Francis). She managed to convince Ralph Waldo Emerson and Nathaniel Hawthorne, among others, to back her research. She even managed to convince the vicar who oversaw Shakespeare's grave to allow her to open the grave to find the evidence she was sure was buried there. But at the last moment she lost her nerve to have his body exhumed. She ultimately lost her mind as well and died in an insane asylum.

Ignatius Donnelly, the American politician who popularized the idea of the lost continent of Atlantis, wrote a book in which he claimed to find that Bacon had hidden ciphers about himself in the Shakespeare plays to prove his authorship. Bacon was known to be interested in cryptograms and ciphers, and many other codes. Donnelly believed the key to Bacon's identity was coded into the plays. By the end of the nineteenth century there were many Baconian societies and publications concerned about interpeting the alleged codes.

Other candidates to have written under Shakespeare's name have been the playwright Christopher Marlowe, The Earl of Oxford, Sir Walter Raleigh and a woman by the name of Anne Whateley who may once have been engaged to the young Shakespeare, but never married him. Every few years, it seems, there is yet another theory about who really wrote Shakespeare's plays.

Despite all the gaps in our knowledge and unless some much better evidence to the contrary turns up, it is probably safe to conclude that the man who wrote *as* Shakespeare *was* Shakespeare.

II.
Places

ATLANTIS

The story of the "lost continent" of Atlantis begins with the Greek philosopher Plato. About 355 B.C., when Plato was more than seventy years old, he began writing a series of works in which the story of Atlantis was to figure prominently. According to Plato, Atlantis was an island continent, somewhere out in the Atlantic, and had been the home to a great civilization. But the Atlanteans had become decadent and greedy, and the gods decided to punish them. The island continent sank and vanished ". . . in one terrible day and night."

According to Plato this had happened a long time ago, and the story had been told to one of his kinsmen by an Egyptian priest. Even the Greeks considered the Egyptians a very ancient people.

Plato was a philosopher, not a historian, and though he insisted he was recounting "authentic history," he often made up stories to drive home a philosophical point. Atlantis is not mentioned in any other Greek literature or any other ancient literature at all. Plato's most famous pupil, Aristotle, didn't believe there had been a real Atlantis, and the subject was almost completely ignored for many centuries.

It was the European discovery of America that brought the Atlantis idea to the forefront once again. Some speculated that America was Atlantis or at least that Plato had heard rumors of America. For over 200 years a few stubborn mapmakers insisted on labeling America "Atlantis."

Some insisted that the Maya and Incas were really refugees from Atlantis.

A nineteenth-century American politician and crank scholar, Ignatius T. Donnelly, wrote a very influential book in which he claimed that Atlantis was the original homeland of all civilizations. Nazi-influenced scholars tried to prove that Atlantis was the original home of the Aryan race, while some Englishmen insist that Atlantis was really Britain.

The American mystic Edgar Cayce, who died in 1945, placed Atlantis somewhere off the coast of Florida. One of Cayce's

One of many early maps showing the "lost continent" of Atlantis.

pet prophecies was that the sunken continent would rise again by the end of the decade of the 1960s, and that this event would trigger a chain of worldwide geological catastrophes. Some of Cayce's followers claimed they found evidence that Atlantis was actually rising, and for a few months in late 1968 and early 1969 Cayce followers genuinely feared that the catastrophes were about to begin. However, recently they have been rather quiet about this prediction.

This just scratches the surface of the speculation about Atlantis. Geologists insist that there never was a continent in the middle of the Atlantic, and there never could have been.

During the early 1980s some scientists believed they had finally solved the puzzle. They found evidence of a massive volcanic explosion that destroyed the island of Thera in the Aegean off the coast of Greece. They said the thick ash fall from the explosion helped to bring down the powerful Minoan civilization. The explosion took place around 1400 B.C., long before Plato lived. But they believed Plato used an exaggerated and garbled account of the explosion as the basis for his Atlantis story.

More recently, that theory has been losing supporters because it has not been possible to connect the volcanic explosion with the fall of the Minoans.

The latest, but certainly not the last, "solution" to the Atlantis mystery comes from Dr. Eberhard Zangger, a geoarchaeologist, in his 1992 book, *The Flood from Heaven*. According to Dr. Zangger, Plato must have gotten hold of an ancient Egyptian account of the fall of Troy, and therefore Atlantis is really Troy.

LEMURIA AND MU

Humans have always longed to have things neat and symmetrical. Thus when Europeans sailed into the Atlantic Ocean and found the continents of North America and South America, many assumed that similar continents would be found in the Pacific. Mapmakers often inserted an ill-defined land mass, which they labeled *Terra Australis Incognita,* or "the great unknown southern continent." A small continent that we now call Australia was indeed found in the South Pacific, but that didn't really satisfy the desire for symmetry.

When it finally became absolutely clear that no great southern continent existed, many refused to give up on the idea and simply assumed the continent had been "lost," a sort of Atlantis of the Pacific.

Lemuria, the most enduring name for the lost Pacific continent, was first proposed by an English zoologist named Philip L. Schlater. He was trying to figure out how the same form of monkeylike lemur could be found in Madagascar, Africa, India and Indonesia. He proposed that all of these areas were once connected by a vast continent he called Lemuria and which had since disappeared.

A German naturalist named Ernst Heinrich Haeckel was more daring. He proposed that Lemuria was the "cradle of the human race."

Modern geologists have shown that no such continent ever existed nor is such a continent necessary to explain the distribution of plant and animal life. The continents as we know them were once connected, but they broke apart and "drifted" away from one another, carrying animal and plant life with them.

While any shred of scientific justification for a lost continent in the Pacific disappeared long ago, the concept had been accepted by mystics and crank scholars, and they did not give up so easily. The racist theories of the Scottish mythologist Lewis Spence held that white refugees from a sinking Lemuria brought civilization to the rest of the world.

James Churchward, whose works were popular in the 1920s and still enjoy a small following today, called the great unknown southern continent Mu. The name was based on a mistranslation of some Mayan hieroglyphics. According to Churchward, "The dominant race in the land of Mu was a white race."

A Newburgh, New York, spiritualist named John Ballou wrote what he claimed was an angelically inspired new bible called *Oahspe*. Ballou called the lost Pacific continent Pan, and once again the familiar theme of the supremacy of the white race appears.

In the 1940s the popular science fiction magazine *Amazing Stories* ran a series of tales by a Pennsylvania welder named Richard S. Shaver. They allegedly told the authentic story of the Earth beginning at a time when both Atlantis and Lemuria towered above the waves. The first story in the series was titled "I Remember Lemuria." It was claimed that Shaver could tap his "racial memory" to reconstruct Earth's lost history.

Lemuria has had nowhere near the popularity of Atlantis, but some people still believe in the lost Pacific continent, no matter what name it is given.

THE MONEY PIT

The site of the longest-running, most mysterious and certainly most frustrating treasure hunt in history is on Oak Island, a small island off the coast of the Canadian province of Nova Scotia.

In the summer of 1795 a Nova Scotia farm boy named Daniel McGinnis rowed out to the island for a bit of exploring. He found a clearing that contained a large oak tree and beneath it a saucer-shaped depression. His first thought was of buried treasure, for he had heard stories that the notorious pirate Captain Kidd had hidden his stolen hoard somewhere in the vicinity.

The next day the boy was back with two friends, and they started digging with gusto. Just two feet under the surface they encountered a layer of flagstones that protected the top of a circular shaft that had been dug out and then refilled with dirt. Ten feet below the stones was a layer of oak logs. Ten feet further was another layer of logs, and then another. The digging was backbreaking work, and finally, exhausted and frustrated, the boys gave up.

The farm boys were just the first of a long series of treasure hunters who, over the years, have come up with some mysterious and tantalizing clues, but no treasure. Six men have lost their lives in various accidents connected with the Oak Island dig, and the expeditions have cost millions of dollars. This has earned the spot the name the Money Pit, not for the money it is supposed to contain but for all the money that has been poured into the attempt to solve its mysteries.

In 1803 diggers discovered that at the depth of 93 feet the pit filled with water that could not be pumped out. Fifty years later another expedition found out why. This was no simple hole in the ground. The pit was connected to the shore by an elaborate system of drains and tunnels. The digging destroyed the barrier that held back the seawater.

Various expeditions have come up with a few artifacts, some links of chain, a carved bone bosun's whistle, a scrap of parchment. Coconut fiber has also been found, though the nearest coconut tree is 1,500 miles away.

In 1971 a TV camera was lowered 230 feet into the pit and caught an image of what appeared to be a severed human hand, well preserved by the salt water and lack of oxygen. Further attempts to locate the hand were unsuccessful.

All the digging and the water have so weakened the area around the Money Pit that it has collapsed, creating a huge depression. The treasure, if treasure there be, must have been shifted well out of its original position and will be harder to locate than ever.

There isn't a clue as to who dug the original pit or what it was meant to conceal. It was an elaborate and time-consuming engineering task that seems well beyond the abilities of a band of pirates. According to one theory the pit was constructed in about 1780 by army engineers under the orders of Sir Henry Clinton, commander of the British forces in America, to hide money that had been placed in his care. It is an attractive idea, but no additional evidence supports it.

For two centuries the Money Pit has kept its secret.

THE SARGASSO SEA

A vast area of the central North Atlantic Ocean has been named for the seaweed sargassum (*sargaco* in Portuguese) found there in abundance. Since the time of Columbus, the Sargasso Sea has had an ominous and mysterious reputation.

The circulation of the ocean is such that seaweed as well as other debris from anywhere in the Atlantic may be carried by currents into the relatively calm center of the area. It is also a region where the wind can die for long stretches. Sailing ships were often becalmed there.

The first mariner we know of to sail right through the Sargasso Sea was Columbus. He had some odd experiences there (his compass appeared to go awry and he saw some unexplained lights) but they did not bother him very much. Later, sailors began to tell tales of terror about the region. It was said the weed was so thick that ships would become stuck, and men on board would die from thirst under the broiling sun.

It was a ships' graveyard according to some, a place where wrecks and derelict ships from all over the world were carried to drift aimlessly amid the weeds until they rotted and sank. In legend it was a place haunted by the ghosts of dead sailors and the home of all manner of terrifying sea monsters.

The Sargasso Sea was used as a background by adventure novelists and later by filmmakers and cartoonists, but the legends about the region are mostly just that. While a good deal of seaweed is in the area, much of it from the Caribbean and the Gulf of Mexico, there is nowhere enough to stop a ship. Today more oil and tar from oil spills than sargassum can be found in the Sargasso Sea. A derelict ship, like any other piece of debris, would most likely be caught by the currents and drift into the Sargasso Sea. A ship would also tend to stay afloat longer than in stormier latitudes. But even in the Sargasso Sea, a derelict ship was a rarity. The most dangerous creatures of the region were not monsters, but borer worms, which would attack a becalmed ship and eat into its wooden hull.

The Sargasso Sea encompassed what later became known as the Bermuda Triangle, and the Triangle seems to have inherited some of the older mystery, as well as the general feeling, that this was a place where the ordinary laws of nature were suspended.

THE BERMUDA TRIANGLE

For centuries, people have believed that mysterious and terrible things, particularly disappearances, happen frequently in certain areas of the sea. The most recent manifestation of this ancient belief is the Bermuda Triangle.

The term itself is not ancient. It was coined in 1964 by writer Vincent Gaddes in *Argosy* magazine to denote a triangular area, with the east coast of Florida as one point of the triangle, Puerto Rico as another, and the island of Bermuda as the third. Gaddes said a large number of mysterious disappearances took place in that area.

While hundreds of mysterious disappearances have been attributed to the Triangle, the key case is the disappearance of Flight 19. On December 5, 1945, five TBF Avengers took off on a routine training mission from Fort Lauderdale Naval Air Station. Two hours after the flight began, and at about the time the planes should have been on their way back home, the Fort Lauderdale base began picking up messages indicating that the men of the flight were lost and confused. Their instruments did not seem to be working properly. Shortly after 4 P.M. all communication with the flight was lost.

Search operations were begun immediately, during which one search plane, a Martin Mariner, also disappeared. No trace of the five Avengers or their fourteen crew members was ever found. No official explanation for the disappearance was ever given.

Gaddes may have been prompted to write his article by the disappearance, early in 1963, of the *Marine Sulphur Queen,* a large tanker. On February 4, 1963, she sent a routine radio call from a position approximately 279 miles west off Key West and was never heard from again. A few life jackets and bits of debris were found, but nothing more.

Perhaps the spookiest story associated with the Triangle is that of the *Carroll A. Deering.* The five-masted schooner was found beached and abandoned near Cape Hatteras, North Carolina, on January 30, 1921. Nothing indicated what had happened to the crew. Though Cape Hatteras is not in the Bermuda Triangle, the ship had sailed through the area, and many assumed that the crew vanished there.

Many, many other disappearances are attributed to the Bermuda Triangle, some genuinely mysterious, others exaggerated. Ships do sink and planes do crash, sometimes for reasons not at all mysterious.

In addition to the actual disappearances, all sorts of vague stories persist about strange phenomena in the area. Compasses are supposed to go awry, strange lights are seen and UFOs and even sea monsters are allegedly spotted there.

Skeptics argue that given the amount of sea and air traffic through the Bermuda Triangle area (it contains some of the

76

In 1945, five fighter planes like those pictured above disappeared in the Bermuda Triangle.

world's busiest sea and air lanes) no unusually large number of disappearances, mysterious or otherwise, has occurred. As for the wilder accounts about UFOs, etc., there is simply no evidence to back them up.

Exaggeration and poor reporting, say the skeptics, played a large part in the building of the Bermuda Triangle legend. Regarding the key case of Flight 19, most books say the flight took place in perfect weather and the flight leader was an experienced pilot. In fact, the weather was poor and the flight leader made a series of small but ultimately disastrous errors. What really happened is that the flight became lost, and the pilots were forced to ditch their planes in the darkness in a stormy sea when they ran out of fuel. However, a 1992 report that the wreckage of the five planes had been located on the ocean floor proved to be wrong.

THE GREAT PYRAMID

By any measure, the Great Pyramid at Giza, just outside of Cairo, Egypt, is one of the most awesome man-made structures in world history. It is certainly the greatest and most durable construction of the ancient world. For centuries it has excited wonder and speculation. The Great Pyramid has always had mystical associations. The pyramid, topped by the all-seeing eye, is the most puzzling part of the great seal of the United States. It's right there on the back of a dollar bill.

Actually, three large pyramids are located in Giza, and loads of others are scattered throughout the Egyptian desert. But it is the largest of the pyramids—The Great Pyramid—that captures the imagination.

Of this much we can be reasonably certain: The pyramid was built around 2569 B.C. as a tomb for the king known as Khufu. The Egyptians had experimented with pyramid-shaped tombs before, but Khufu's pyramid, which is as tall as a forty-story building, was far and away their most ambitious project. Most of the two and a half million blocks of limestone and granite that make up the pyramid were quarried close at hand. Some may have been floated down the Nile on rafts from where they were quarried.

Genuine mysteries surround the pyramid's construction. How, for example, were blocks, some weighing as much as seventy tons, piled tier upon tier? The most popular explanation is that the builders constructed an enormous ramp of mud and rubble and dragged the stones up on rollers. The builders must have had a fairly sophisticated knowledge of geometry to calculate the proper angle at which a pyramid could be built without the blocks sliding off.

While the exact building techniques cannot be determined today, some 4,500 years after the pyramid was built, most Egyptologists do not believe they were beyond the abilities of the Egyptians. The real key to building the Great Pyramid, and all the other pyramids, was the Egyptian kings' ability to organize huge work forces over a long period of time. The Great Pyramid may have been built over a period of thirty years. It was the Egyptians' organizational genius as much as their engineering genius that must be admired.

But many have looked at the Great Pyramid and decided that the Egyptians, with their simple tools and techniques, could not have possibly constructed so magnificent an edifice. Some believed that the ancient Hebrews built the pyramid. A few have insisted that Noah himself, after overseeing construction of the ark, went on to direct work on the Great Pyramid. Still others have said it was built by refugees from the great lost civilization of Atlantis, and in more recent times it has been credited to superintelligent extraterrestrials.

The Great Pyramid.

Not a shred of evidence supports any of these wilder claims. There is absolutely no doubt that the Great Pyramid and all the other pyramids of Egypt were built by the Egyptians. Nor is there any reason to believe that the Egyptians possessed a now lost secret of levitation or any other magical secrets that made building the pyramid easier.

Considerable speculation has also been aired as to what the purpose of the Great Pyramid was. Clearly it was a tomb for the pharaoh or king. But was it also used as some sort of astronomical observatory? Probably not, but that question is still open.

Then there is the theory that the Great Pyramid is some sort of repository for all manner of ancient wisdom. A surprisingly large number of people have believed that by interpreting various measurements in the pyramid one could calculate the distance from the Earth to the Sun or the frequency of eclipses. A whole "science" called pyramidology grew up around this belief. Some pyramidologists said that by interpreting measurements one could even predict the future. Scientists and scholars refer to people who hold such views as "pyramidiots."

Still, the Great Pyramid is such a monumental achievement that it continues to excite wonder and speculation.

THE REALM OF KING ARTHUR

Traditionally we picture King Arthur and his Knights of the Round Table clanking about in medieval suits of armor. However, historical research into the origins of the tales of King Arthur, which has been extensive, indicates that the historical Arthur lived in the late fifth century, and that makes him a figure of the Dark Ages, not medieval times.

The late fifth century was a time when the Christian and Romanized Celts who inhabited the British Isles were being overrun by barbarian Saxon invaders. Arthur was probably a war leader who managed to rouse the sagging spirits of his badly defeated countrymen and win a series of impressive victories against the Saxons. One theory is that his success was due to his knowledge of the Roman arts of war, particularly the use of armored horsemen. At best Arthur would have worn an iron cap and a mail shirt, and his horse might have been lightly armored. Still, the barbaric Saxons would have nothing comparable. When medieval writers took up the Arthur stories, they merely dressed the hero in the fighting garb of their own time. Arthur was killed around 540, not by the Saxons, but in a dispute with members of his own family.

Where was Camelot? Visitors to the romantic ruins of Tintagel Castle in Cornwall are led to believe that they are standing in Camelot's remains. However, the castle was not built until a full seven hundred years after Arthur lived, and nothing on the site goes back to Arthurian times. Besides, authentic Arthurian traditions are not associated with Cornwall.

Sir Thomas Malory, who wrote the most influential of the Arthurian romances *Le Morte d'Arthur,* placed Camelot at Winchester. A fine castle stands at Winchester, and the famous Round Table, or at least *a* famous round table, is on display in the great hall. However, the Round Table is a sixteenth-century fake, old enough to make it a genuine antique, but not old enough for Arthur.

The most probable site for Camelot is a place called Cadbury Hill, which has been used as a fortress since the Stone Age. Archaeologists found that it had been heavily refortified during Arthur's time. It is located near a stream once called Cam—which means crooked in Celtic. That may have been the origin of the name Camelot.

Cadbury is near the ruins of Glastonbury Abbey, long rumored to be the burial place of Arthur. The tomb of King Arthur and his queen were said to have been located there in the twelfth century. In 1278 the remains were removed to a more impressive burial site, which survived until the abbey was dissolved in 1539. However the whole story of finding King Arthur's tomb was probably a hoax cooked up by the monks who were trying to raise money to restore their abbey after a disastrous fire.

But the tradition that places Arthur's burial at Glastonbury may still be valid. Arthur's final and fatal battle was supposed to have been fought at Camlan. Once again there is an association with the River Cam.

In the legend, Arthur was not really killed but was carried off to the mythical Isle of Avalon, where he "sleeps" until needed to lead his people once again. Glastonbury was once a series of hills surrounded by a marshy lowland. It could easily have been considered an island.

Arthur may have been buried secretly so that news of his death would not hearten his enemies and discourage his followers. Later the story would spread that he was only "sleeping."

King Arthur and his realm may not have been as grand as later chroniclers depicted them—but they were quite real.

EASTER ISLAND

On Easter Sunday, 1722, the Dutch explorer Jacob Roggeveen landed on a small island in the South Pacific, previously unknown to Europeans. The inhabitants of the island called it Rapa Nui, but Roggeveen called it Easter Island, and that is the name by which it is known today.

The inhabitants of the island were Polynesians, a people who lived on a large number of South Pacific islands, though this one was by far the most remote. The population of the island seemed small and impoverished. Yet the island itself contained hundreds of huge and very curious-looking stone statues. Many of the statues had been knocked down or fallen over—many others were unfinished or had been abandoned near the quarries where they had been carved.

The inhabitants of Easter Island showed little interest in these remarkable monuments, and it seemed inconceivable that they could have ever created them.

Contact with Europeans was a disaster for the Easter Island natives. Many were carried off into slavery. The few that managed to return carried the smallpox virus, a disease for which the people of Easter Island had no immunity. By 1877 only 111 island natives survived out of the thousands that once lived there. They were converted to Christianity and lost touch with whatever fragments of their heritage they still remembered.

The Easter Island statues remained a mystery, and all sorts of romantic fantasies were spun around them. The most persistent was that the statues had been built by some vanished super race, perhaps from the lost continents of Atlantis or Lemuria. The truth, pieced together by investigations over the years, is less romantic.

The Polynesians were great seafarers, but Easter Island is so remote that those who settled on it were cut off from contact with other islands, and so they developed their own culture similar to, but not identical with, that of other Polynesian islands.

An illustration from an early travel book showing eighteenth century sailors visiting Easter Island before the giant statues had been toppled. (New York Public Library)

Many Polynesians made large statues that were set around burial grounds or other sacred sites. These were usually made of wood and soon rotted. There was little wood on Easter Island but plenty of volcanic rock could be found. Modern tests have shown that the rock can be sculpted with the simple tools that would have been available to Easter Island natives. They could have dragged the statues from the mountain quarries to the places along the shore where they were set up, though they weighed many tons. It would have taken a lot of time and effort, and a larger population than Roggeveen encountered, but it would have been possible. No need to invoke unknown supercivilizations.

For a thousand years or more Easter Island had a large and thriving population. They built statues, altars and other monuments. Then at some point, about a century before the arrival of the Europeans, something happened. Perhaps it was rivalries among various clan groups, perhaps a revolt; no one is sure. Statues were thrown down and many being built were abandoned unfinished. In the chaos that followed, Easter Island culture collapsed, and what Roggeveen encountered was the diminished and dispirited remnant of a once thriving culture.

Easter Island and its inhabitants still have plenty of mysteries, such as the "talking boards" tablets or rods of wood inscribed with a form of writing that can no longer be interpreted. Only a handful of the tablets still exist, and they completely baffle linguists. And there is the curious "bird man," a figure found inscribed throughout the island. It once had great meaning to the people of Easter Island. Today no one knows what it means.

THE EMPTY GRAVE

In the spring of 1939 archaeologists began digging into a one-hundred-foot-long barrow, or mound, at Sutton Hoo in the part of England called East Anglia. Such barrows usually covered burial sites. Archaeologists thought or rather hoped that this barrow might contain an Anglo-Saxon ship that had been buried along with the remains of the chieftain who had owned it. Ship burials were common among the Vikings and not unknown among their close relatives in the British Isles.

Such burials often contained archaeologically interesting but otherwise unspectacular material. Though there had been rumors of buried treasure—as there always are in such cases—but none of the diggers imagined, even in their wildest dreams, that this mound would really contain a treasure.

But it did. Inside the ribs of the decayed ship the diggers uncovered dozens of pieces of beautifully worked gold jewelry encrusted with precious stones. They found gold coins and ingots, a jewel-studded sword and—the greatest find of all—a magnificent gold and silver inlayed helmet decorated with dragons and battle scenes. The diggers discovered some Christian artifacts such as silver spoons and bowls that would have been used in church services, but this was essentially a pagan burial. Sutton Hoo was far and away the greatest find of its type ever made in Britain. The treasure is now on display in the British Museum.

The king (because of the richness of the find it was assumed that the burial was a royal one) was laid to rest in the ship that would carry him to the afterlife, and he would be accompanied by all the treasures he would need in the next world. He was buried during a period when this part of Britain, while nominally Christian, was still basically a pagan land.

Some coins found in the barrow fixed the date of the burial at around 625 to 630, the darkest of the Dark Ages. Nothing indicated who was buried in the tomb or that anyone was buried there at all. And *that* is the mystery. No trace of bones or any other human remains were found. The very acid soil may have destroyed organic remains, but most scholars believe the burial mound at Sutton Hoo never contained a body. They speculate that the king's body may have been lost at sea, but his subjects carried out the traditional burial rites anyway.

NOAH'S ARK

The story of Noah and the flood is one of the best-known stories in the Bible. It contains these words: "And the ark rested in the seventh month, upon the seventeenth day of the month, upon the mountains of Ararat."

For centuries people have been trying to find the place where the ark finally came to rest. It has been a search filled with extraordinary difficulties. First, the location given in the Bible is not very specific, for the term Ararat describes a large area, including parts of modern-day Turkey, Syria, Iran, Iraq and Armenia. Several mountains in this region have traditionally been regarded as the resting place of the ark. Most modern

The French artist Gustave Dore pictured the earth as being littered with human bodies after the flood receded.

seekers of Noah's ark have concentrated their efforts on a tall mountain in Turkey known locally as Agri Dagi but known throughout much of the western world as Mount Ararat.

This mountain overlooks Turkey's border with Iran and what was until recently Soviet Armenia. The mountain itself is difficult to climb, and since the region is politically unstable, there have been times when all expeditions have been banned. Explorers have often been threatened by bandits. The mountain is also covered by glaciers, which means any object that had come to rest there thousands of years ago would probably be frozen into the ice and also could have been transported a considerable distance down the mountain by the glaciers' movement. This would make the ark far more difficult to locate than if it were just sitting on the surface. Still, Mount Ararat is by no means unexplored territory. While many of those who have climbed the mountain say they have found no trace of Noah's ark, others insist they have found it, though even the best of the claims have not been substantiated.

In the past, pieces of wood and pitch, the material used to make boats watertight, that was said to have come from Noah's ark were venerated as holy relics or sold as charms against a variety of evils. However, the manufacture of phoney holy relics was a thriving business until the late eighteenth century.

Most scientists regard the story of Noah's ark as allegorical rather than a literal truth, thus they see any search for the ark as a hopeless task. In modern times most of those who have taken part in or funded searches for Noah's ark are fundamentalist Christians out to prove the literal truth of the Bible. However, stories report that in the 1850s a group of British scientists found the ark but suppressed the information because it did not fit into their nonreligious views. Another story says that a Russian expedition found the ark just before the Russian Revolution, but that all news of the discovery was later hidden by the officially atheist government of the Soviet Union. However, no authentic records of either of these alleged expeditions have ever been found.

In 1955 an expedition headed by French industrialist Fernand

Navarra brought back fragments of what appeared to be hand-worked wood from the heights of Mount Ararat. He said they were from a wooden ship buried deep in the ice. Some estimated that the wood was several thousand years old, but radiocarbon dating put the age at about twelve hundred years, far too recent to have been part of Noah's ark.

Aerial photographs of what appear to be a ship or structure of some sort high on Mount Ararat have been given widely differing interpretations. The type of evidence that would convince those not already convinced of the ark's existence has yet to be produced. But it is safe to predict that this quest will continue.

EL DORADO

When the Spanish conquered Mexico and then Peru, an enormous quantity of gold came into their possession. Suddenly, men who had been poor soldiers became as wealthy as kings. The dream of instant golden wealth fired the imagination of generations, and not only of those in Spain. Throughout Europe men dreamed that other golden civilizations in addition to the Aztecs and Incas were ripe for plunder. And rumors always led them to believe such a dream might be true.

The most persistent and compelling of the stories was that of *el hombre dorado,* the gilded man. The story was that once a year the king of a land somewhere in Central America or South America covered himself with a sticky substance and then rolled in gold dust. Completely covered, the gilded king got into a canoe on the shores of a lake, paddled off into the center and jumped into the water to wash off the gold dust. When he did this, the crowd that had gathered on the shore sent up a great cheer, which signaled the start of a feast.

The story of El Dorado, as both the king and the land itself came to be called, took so powerful a grip on the imaginations of generations of treasure seekers that no amount of hardship or disappointment could break it. It also resulted in terrible suffering for the natives who were tortured and killed in great numbers by those looking for the fabled land.

The first expedition to find El Dorado was launched in 1529. El Dorado continued to appear in various places on maps well into the eighteenth century. The great natural scientist and traveler Alexander von Humboldt finally put an end to the fantasy at the beginning of the nineteenth century. He conducted an extensive reconnaissance of South America and Central America, retracing the routes of most of the El Dorado seekers, and found what they found—nothing.

Ironically, the El Dorado story was really based on fact, and the land of the gilded king was actually located by three separate expeditions in February 1539. But they refused to believe it, because the land they found contained no gold.

The ceremony had been performed by the chibcha people who lived on a high, nearly inaccessible plateau called Cundinamarca, in what is now Columbia. What the El Dorado seekers had never bothered to ask themselves was, "How much gold dust does it take to cover a man's body?" The answer is "not much." The Chibchas got the small amount they needed by trading with other tribes. But even that had strained their limited resources, and the ceremony had been abandoned some forty years before the treasure hunters arrived.

NAZCA DRAWINGS

On the surface of a high plateau on the coast of Peru, are drawings so enormous that they can be appreciated only from an airplane. Yet they were made centuries before any airplanes existed.

The area is called the Nazca Desert, and it is virtually rainless. Thus figures etched into the surface would survive for centuries. Occasionally, travelers through the region would notice the strange and obviously artificial lines on the desert floor, but the lines were unimpressive and meaningless at ground level. However, starting in the 1950s, as planes began to pass over the Nazca region, air travelers saw that some of the lines formed parts of gigantic figures. Aerial photographs proved to be highly dramatic.

A variety of figures—birds, spiders, fish, even a monkey—and a couple unidentifiable creatures can be seen. Rectangular shapes and a large number of straight lines or "roads" apparently run from nowhere to nowhere. The surface on which the figures and lines are incised is made of gravel and pebbles. To make a line, rocks and pebbles were moved to expose the lighter soil beneath. The rocks were then piled up on each side of the line.

No one is exactly sure who made the drawings, but the best guess is that they were made some fifteen hundred years ago by a pre-Inca people called the Nazcas—after whom the desert was named. Some of the figures look like those found on Nazca

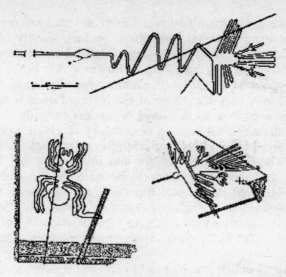

Diagrams of some of the Nazca drawings.

pottery. The Incas, who conquered the Nazcas, had no respect for the figures. They built a road that cuts right through them. Neither the Nazcas nor the Incas had a written language, and the Nazcas themselves were completely wiped out after the Spanish conquest of Peru. This page of history is now blank.

The figures would not have been difficult to make. Still they would have required a great deal of time and labor, so they must have meant a great deal to the people who made them. But what did they mean?

An American scholar, Paul Koosk, was one of the first to become interested in the Nazca drawings. He thought that the lines pointed to certain astronomical alignments. He said the lines represented "the largest astronomy book in the world." After Koosk's death others tried to take up his work, but the astronomical significance of the lines has not been accepted by most scientists and scholars.

The most sensational explanation of all for the Nazca lines

and drawings is that they were used as markers on landing fields for extraterrestrial spaceships. In fact, shortly after they were discovered, they were jokingly dubbed "prehistoric landing fields." The dry lake bed at Edwards Air Force Base in California, on which the space shuttle generally lands, has lines on it that look very like those of the Nazca. Edwards Air Force Base, however, has no drawings of spiders or birds.

The extraterrestrial landing field theory received much popular attention in the 1970s, but scientists never took it seriously. No one knows what the figures and lines were for. The best guess is that they were made to be seen by the gods of the Nazca who lived in the sky. But that's only a guess.

STONEHENGE

The first thing that one must recognize about Stonehenge, the enormous circle of stones on Salisbury Plain in England, is that it is not an isolated mystery.

Stonehenge is only the best known of what are called megalithic monuments found throughout Britain and on many parts of the European continent. The monuments are also similar to some found in Asia, North America and elsewhere.

Stonehenge was first mentioned in writing in the twelfth century, though it is much older than that. According to the chronicler, the name meant "hanging stones" because some of the stones seem to "hang as it were in the air." That was probably a reference to the stones perched upon the tops of the great upright stones. That is certainly the feature of Stonehenge that

Stonehenge as it appeared in the eighteenth century.

first strikes the modern visitor, and more of these stones were in place back in the twelfth century.

Since no one knew who built Stonehenge or why, people began to make up stories. According to one account, it was a place where condemned criminals were hung. According to another, it was a monument constructed by King Arthur's uncle with the help of the magician Merlin. Others said it was built by the Romans. The Romans had conquered the area, and they certainly had the technical ability to construct such a monument. But it is quite unlike anything the Romans ever built anywhere else. They must have seen it, though they do not mention it in their records. The Romans, who had very definite ideas about what monuments should look like, were clearly unimpressed by this circle of stones.

Stonehenge is most frequently associated with the druids— the priests of the ancient Celts. It was supposed to be a place where the druids performed their ceremonies and human sacrifices. But the evidence tells a different story. The druids had nothing to do with Stonehenge. Their ceremonies were conducted in sacred groves, not stone circles.

Stonehenge predates the druids by many centuries. Construction began at the site some five thousand years ago. Builders made additions and alterations over several thousand years. Ultimately it fell into disuse and was abandoned. Its original builders and purpose were forgotten.

The nameless builders of Stonehenge were technologically primitive, but they didn't need Merlin's magic to build the monument. All they needed were simple tools and an enormous expenditure of time and energy. They probably dragged the largest stones over land on sledges and rollers and set them up by means of ropes and levers. Some stones came from a mountain range in Wales, over one hundred miles away from the site. Builders probably floated these down on rafts.

The most difficult question about Stonehenge: What was it used for? Why would a people, or in this case several different peoples, decide to put so much time and effort into building a monument? What did it mean to them? Many answers have been suggested for these questions.

The most common explanation is that Stonehenge was a temple, though no one is sure what sort of worship went on there. It may have had something to do with worship of the Sun, for if you stand in the center of Stonehenge on the morning of the summer solstice, the longest day of the year, you can see the Sun rise directly over a very prominent and ancient stone in the circle.

In 1963 Gerald Hawkins, a well-known astronomer, suggested that the monument had all sorts of other possible astronomical alignments that would have been extremely useful in determining the length of a year and even in calculating the cycle of eclipses. This theory received a lot of attention from the general public, but professional archaeologists remained unconvinced.

Another suggestion is that the monument is really the remains of a fort or other military structure.

With all the conflicting theories and lack of real, solid evidence, we can only repeat what one observer wrote over two hundred years ago: "God knows what their [the stones] use was."

96

THE MYSTERY TOWER

Presumed Viking artifacts have been found up and down the east coast of America and farther inland as well. Of these, the most visually impressive is the Mystery Tower, which stands in a park in Newport, Rhode Island. In fact, the tower is the official symbol of the town, which is best known for the fabulous mansions of some of its wealthy inhabitants.

The Mystery Tower is a curious-looking structure. It appears to be the stone shell of a building about twenty-four feet tall. In the early years of the nineteenth century the structure was generally called the Old Stone Mill of Governor Benedict Arnold. But as enthusiasm for a Norse discovery of North America grew, many began to identify the tower as a Viking structure that was perhaps the remains of a stone church. While most scholars did not accept the Viking identification, it did take a powerful hold on the popular imagination. It was one of the inspirations for Henry Wadsworth Longfellow's poem *The Skeleton in Armor* about the discovery of a Viking skeleton in North America. The poem was required reading in many schools right into the middle of the twentieth century.

A major revival of support for the Norse origin of the stone tower began with a book called *Newport Tower,* written by amateur archaeologist Philip Ainsworth and published in 1942.

The controversy probably could have been settled by archaeological excavations around the tower site, but for years the Park

Commission of Newport flatly refused permission for any sort of dig. They feared the famous monument would be damaged.

Finally in 1948 the Park Commission did allow excavations under the direction of Harvard University and the Peabody Museum. The excavations showed that the tower was just what most people originally thought it was: an early colonial structure, though it predated Governor Arnold by at least a century. This did not entirely dim its luster or clear up the mystery. The tower, built around 1650, is one of the oldest buildings still standing in continental North America. And no one is exactly sure who built it or what it was used for.

THE KINGDOM OF PRESTER JOHN

Today, few people have ever heard of Prester John, or John the Priest King. But to the people of Europe during the Middle Ages, the Kingdom of Prester John was as real as China.

Rumors of a great and powerful Christian kingdom located somewhere in Central Asia and led by John the Priest King began circulating in Europe early in the twelfth century. It was a time when the expanding power of Islam was pushing back Christianity and it seemed as if the Moslems were ready to invade Europe itself. According to rumors, the Christian army of Prester John was literally going to ride to the rescue.

At different times a variety of Central Asian rulers, including the Mongol conqueror Genghis Khan, were identified, or to be more accurate misidentified, as Prester John. Pope Alexander III sent a letter to Prester John. Marco Polo was asked to look for him. Unfortunately he did not exist.

By about the fourteenth century Asia had become well enough known in Europe for even the most hopeful to realize that no great Christian kingdom was hidden there. So a Dominican friar named Jordanus de Severac had an inspiration. If Prester John did not live in Asia, then he must live somewhere else—in Central Africa.

As it happened, a Christian Kingdom in Africa was quite mysterious to Europeans—Abyssinia or Ethiopia. The Ethiopian Church is very ancient and had been completely cut off from the rest of the Christian world by the rise of Moslem power in Africa.

Early Portuguese explorers were convinced that the Kingdom of Prester John was in Africa. For decades, maps of Africa continued to refer to Ethiopia as the land of Prester John. The first European book ever written about Ethiopia, which appeared in the fifteenth century, referred to the king of that land as Prester John or simply "the Preste."

The Ethiopian monarchs resented the identification. They traced their heritage all the way back to Solomon and Sheba's son Menelik and proudly pointed out that they possessed a whole string of titles far more exalted than that of priest.

After the fifteenth century, the identification of Ethiopia with the Kingdom of Prester John became untenable, and with no further places left to locate the kingdom, the long-running legend finally expired. But how had it begun?

No one really knows. The best guess is that it started with the Nestorians, a group of eastern Christians who had small communities spread from Syria to China. They told the story of an Indian king named Vizan, a name often translated as John, who had converted to Christianity. There is no evidence that a Christian king ruled in India, but once the story began to circulate it seemed to attach itself to anyplace where there might be any kind of Christian community.

THE CANALS OF MARS

Up until the 1940s it was widely believed, even by some professional astronomers, that the planet Mars was crisscrossed by a network of "canals" quite possibly of artificial origin.

The idea was first advanced in 1877 by the Italian astronomer G. V. Schiaparelli. While observing Mars through his telescope he thought he saw streaks on the face of the planet that had not been reported by any other observer. He called the streaks *canali*, which means "channels," a neutral word. However, when the word was translated into English it came out "canals," which implies an artificial origin.

While many astronomers said they couldn't see any canals, others said that they could. The most influential of them was Percival Lowell, director of one of the world's finest observatories at the time, in Flagstaff, Arizona. Lowell saw a whole spider's web of rigidly geometrical canals. At points where the canals intersected one another, he saw a circular dark spot, which he termed an oasis.

Lowell argued that the canals were of artificial origin and had been constructed by a Martian civilization to irrigate their largely dry planet with water from the melting of the Martian ice caps.

A good deal of scientists opposed this radical idea. But until his death in 1916, Lowell stuck to his guns, and his disciples and admirers carried on after him, mapping the canals.

As telescopes improved, fewer and fewer observers reported

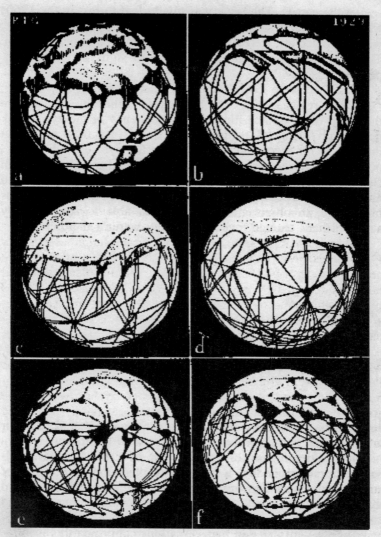

The canals of Mars as mapped by various observers.

seeing the canals. The issue was finally laid to rest in the 1960s when space probes sent back pictures of the Martian surface, which showed a cratered landscape, much like that of the Moon. There were no oases, no canals and no signs of civilization, past or present.

What then were Lowell and the others seeing?

No one really knows. The best guess is that the canals were the result of an optical illusion—the tendency of the eye to link up various disparate features. The eye is far from a perfect instrument for recording reality. Often the eye sees what it expects to see. Even the most passionate defenders of the Martian canals admitted that the lines were extremely faint and hard to interpret. And perhaps once the idea that canals existed was planted in an observer's head, he was able to see them by straining hard enough, even when they weren't there.

THE LEY LINES

In 1921, a sixty-five-year-old English merchant and amateur archaeologist named Alfred Watkins rode to the top of a hill in his native Herefordshire. Looking out over the familiar landscape, he suddenly had a near-mystic vision of a network of straight lines crisscrossing the countryside. These lines passed through ancient stone monuments, earthworks, churches and castles.

Working with detailed maps, Watkins confirmed this inspiration, at least to his own satisfaction. He found that straight lines could connect many prominent natural and man-made features.

This was not accidental; he believed the features marked an ancient system of straight tracks. Where the markers were churches, crosses or other monuments that were not particularly ancient, Watkins concluded that these more modern monuments had replaced ancient monuments or had been put up at pagan holy places. He called the lines "ley" lines because many of the ancient places with names ending in *-ley, -ly* and *-leigh* were found along the straight lines.

Watkins' work inspired a movement that has a small band of devoted and energetic adherents to this day. They call themselves "ley hunters." The belief is most popular in Britain, but ley hunters in other lands have found evidence of the ancient straight tracks in their part of the world as well.

The leys themselves are not physical roads; no actual lines are to be found, and a straight line is not necessarily the best way to get from point A to point B, particularly in a primitive landscape. The leys do not skirt rivers, swamps or other difficult terrain.

If the leys are not physical paths, then what are they? The answer to that question depends on who you consult. In one view they are part of a system of "geomancy" or landscape geometry, "a striking network of lines of subtle force across Britain and elsewhere. . . . understood and marked in prehistoric times by men of wisdom and cosmic consciousness."

Some believe the leys are actually "lines of force" that can be followed with a divining rod.

Most scientists regard the whole idea of leys as loony. They point out that so many different kinds of structures can be used to define a ley, simple chance will allow the dedicated searcher to make many straight lines. Besides, they say, many ley hunters do a lot of fudging. It is sufficient for them if the ley runs near a site, rather than through it.

None of these objections have discouraged the ley hunters. For them the vision of a landscape crisscrossed with ancient straight lines is a totally compelling one.

THE FLAT EARTH

The ancient Greeks had calculated that the Earth is a sphere. During the Middle Ages that idea was lost in Europe for several centuries. However, by the time of Columbus most mariners, like Columbus, assumed the Earth was spherical. Still, many resisted the idea of a spherical Earth even after the globe was circumnavigated by the ships of Ferdinand Magellan.

Often the objections were religious, for certain passages in the Bible, if taken literally, seem to indicate a flat Earth. As late as the 1940s a rigidly fundamentalist group that controlled the town of Zion, Illinois, had the flat Earth as a central part of its doctrine. The group's leader, Wilbur Glenn Voliva, scorned the "so-called fundamentalists (who) strain out the gnat of evolution and swallow the camel of modern astronomy." To Voliva, the Earth was shaped like a pancake, with the North Pole at the center and the South Pole distributed around the circumference. Ships were kept from falling off the edge by a wall of ice.

During the 1930s Voliva traveled around the world several times, but this did not shake his belief a bit. He offered five thousand dollars to anyone who could prove to him that the world was a sphere. He never paid out a cent.

An Englishman named John Hampden also offered five thousand pounds to anyone who could prove the world was a sphere. Alfred Russel Wallace, natural scientist and codiscoverer of the theory of evolution, took up the challenge and won easily. But

Hampden refused to pay and spent the rest of his life trying to make Wallace's life miserable. Not even a jail sentence for harassment could discourage this flat-Earth fanatic. The harassment continued until 1891 when Hampden finally died; it had gone on for over twenty years. It had bankrupted Hampden and left Wallace both financially and emotionally drained.

Today, a few groups are dedicated to spreading the flat-Earth doctrine, but it is difficult to determine if they are actually serious. When the president of the British Flat Earth Society was shown one of the first satellite pictures of the entire Earth taken from space, he looked at it for a moment and said calmly, "It is easy to see how such a picture could fool the untrained eye."

THE HOLLOW EARTH

In the seventeenth century the astronomer Edmund Halley, of comet fame, suggested that the Earth might be like a Chinese puzzle box. There was an outer shell and two inner shells, one the size of Venus and the other the size of Mars, and finally a solid inner core the size of Mercury.

The notion that the Earth was hollow never really caught on until the nineteenth century when it was revived by an American eccentric named John Cleves Symmes. Like Halley, Symmes thought the Earth was made up of concentric spheres. He also said a huge opening, popularly called "Symmes' Hole," was located at each of the poles. The ocean flowed in and out of these openings. The interior of the Earth was supposed to be inhabited. Symmes tried to get the U.S. Congress to finance an expedition to the South Pole to look for the hole, and he nearly succeeded. A stone model of the hollow Earth according to Symmes is atop a memorial in Hamilton, Ohio.

Symmes inspired the science fiction pioneer Jules Verne, who wrote *Journey to the Center of the Earth* in 1864. Edgar Rice Burroughs, creator of Tarzan, wrote a whole cycle of novels set in the hollow Earth.

Symmes inspired more than science fiction writers. Marshall B. Gardner rejected the "absurd notion" of concentric spheres, but enthusiastically endorsed openings at the poles. He said the Earth was completely hollow, and the interior was lit by a small sun about six hundred miles in diameter. Unfortunately, Gardner proposed his theory in 1920, and a few years later Admiral Richard E. Byrd made flights over both the North and South poles. He didn't find any holes.

Still, the idea of the hollow Earth did not die. In the 1940s it was back again in stories by Richard S. Shaver published in the science fiction magazine *Amazing Stories*. Though the stories appeared in a fiction magazine, they were promoted as fact by the magazine's wildman editor, Raymond A. Palmer. Later, Palmer became one of the first people to aggressively promote the existence of flying saucers or UFOs. At one point he claimed that UFOs came from inside the hollow Earth.

Palmer insisted that Admiral Byrd really did discover holes in the poles but the government was covering up this fact. Satellite pictures of the Earth in which no holes appeared had been retouched, Palmer insisted. He also said he had a couple of unretouched photos clearly showing the holes, which had slipped by government censors. All of this and more appeared in a book called *The Hollow Earth,* attributed to a mysterious Dr. Raymond Bernard. It may have been written by Palmer himself. The book is still widely available today.

Undoubtedly the most bizarre theory was put forth by Cyrus Reed Teed who insisted that the Earth is hollow and we are living on the inside! Teed also said he was the new Messiah and adopted the name Koresh. He called his new religion

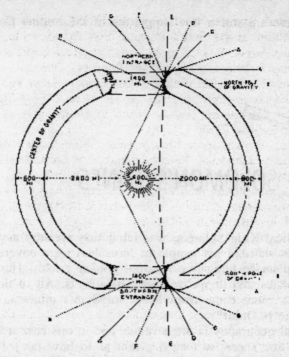

A diagram of the hollow earth. Note the holes at the North and South poles and the small internal sun.

Koreshanity, and the hollow Earth was basic to his faith. Incredibly, he attracted several hundred followers and moved them to Florida, where he died in 1908. The cult he founded lingered for years. The last Koreshanity adherent died in 1983.

Teed's ideas also had some influence among the pseudo-scientists who flourished in Nazi Germany. In 1942 the Nazis actually sent an expedition to the Baltic in hopes of getting pictures of the British fleet by turning their specially adapted cameras skyward to take photos across the center of the hollow Earth.

Though Teed's ideas do now appear to be well and truly

dead, there are still a few supporters of the hollow Earth out there.

KING SOLOMON'S MINES

The biblical King Solomon was fabulously wealthy as well as wise. The walls of his temple in Jerusalem were covered with gold, and inside hung five hundred golden shields. He ate off golden plates and drank from golden goblets. All of this gold and much more came from King Solomon's mines in Ophir. But where is Ophir?

Biblical geography is often vague, and in this case it is maddeningly so. There isn't even a hint as to how far the fabled mines were from Jerusalem or in which direction they were. As a result, treasure hunters have been able to locate Ophir, at least to their own satisfaction, all over the Middle East and Africa.

In the sixteenth century Portuguese traders in East Africa saw what appeared to be the ruins of an ancient city. The native people called the place Great Zimbabwe. Moslem traders who regularly passed through the area said that these were the ruins of King Solomon's mines. The idea did not really catch on in Europe until the mid-nineteenth century when a missionary named Merensky published an account of his visit to what he called the "gold fields of Solomon." Gold in modest amounts had been found in the region. The identification of Great Zimbabwe with Ophir became firmly fixed in Europe. The adventure writer H. Rider Haggard used an African location for his enormously popular novel *King Solomon's Mines*.

The people who lived in the area, however, had always insisted that the ruins were those of a city built by a powerful African kingdom not so very long ago. Europeans who liked to think of Africans as simple tribesmen who lived in huts refused to believe that a native people were capable of such elaborate constructions. But a careful study of the ruins proved beyond any doubt that Great Zimbabwe was indeed built by Africans in the mid-fifteenth century, and it was still inhabited when the Portuguese reached the area. In fact, Portuguese traders had made treaties with the rulers of Great Zimbabwe.

Currently, the most popular candidate for King Solomon's mines is a place called Mahd adh Dhahab in Saudi Arabia. There is evidence that gold was mined there in ancient times, and it is near a trade route that led ultimately to Jerusalem. But the biblical information about Ophir is so sketchy that it is unlikely we will ever know for certain the location of King Solomon's mines.

THE REAL TREASURE ISLAND

When Robert Louis Stevenson wrote *Treasure Island* he almost certainly had Cocos Island in mind. This green speck of a Pacific island off the coast of Central America has, if all the legends are to be believed, been a virtual Swiss bank for pirates. Henry Morgan, William Dampier, and Benito Bonito are just a few of the buccaneers reputed to have deposited their ill-gotten gains on the five-mile-long island.

The most famous or notorious treasure buried on Cocos is

that carried by the *Mary Dear*. In 1820 wealthy Spaniards in Peru loaded an enormous quantity of gold, jewels and other precious objects aboard the British ship to save the wealth from Simon Bolívar's revolutionary army that was advancing on Lima. Only a single soldier was aboard to guard the treasure, and the temptation was too much for the *Mary Dear*'s captain William Thompson. He stole the treasure, and then, according to most accounts, headed for Cocos Island, where he buried it.

Thompson wasn't a particularly clever pirate, and his ship was soon captured by the Spanish. All the crew was hanged except for Thompson and possibly one other man. They saved their necks by promising to lead the Spanish to the hidden treasure. However, one or both of the men managed to escape and hide on the island, and the Spanish never got their treasure back.

After that the murky story gets even murkier. According to the most popular account, Thompson somehow managed to get off the island and wound up in Newfoundland where he died. But on his deathbed he revealed the secret hiding place of the treasure to a man named Keating, who had befriended him. Keating was supposed to have gone to Cocos Island and actually come away with a good deal of treasure. When he died in 1882 he passed the secret on to his wife and three other people. But their forays to the island came up empty.

After that, hordes of treasure seekers armed with what they believed to be Keating's clues or maps pinpointing Benito Bonito's treasure or other treasures have swarmed over the island. Cocos Island is not a tropical paradise. It is unbearably hot, wet and loaded with mosquitoes, snakes and other creatures that do not make good neighbors. Very few people have ever attempted to settle on the island.

In 1904 Earl Fitzwilliam, a wealthy British peer, attacked the island with dynamite. One blast killed a score of workmen and injured Fitzwilliam himself. Franklin Roosevelt, who as a young man was very interested in treasure hunting, visited the island. He found nothing.

A highly romantic illustration of the pirate, Captain Kidd, and his men burying their treasure.

Despite all sorts of rumors and claims of fabulous finds, the only confirmed finds are a couple dozen gold coins that appear to have been dropped at various places rather than buried.

Costa Rica, which owns the island, declared it a national park and has prohibited future digging. So, if any treasure is actually buried on Cocos Island, it is safe for the foreseeable future.

THE LOST DUTCHMAN MINE

Of all the fabulous mines that were found and then somehow supposedly "lost," none has a more romantic or grisly history than the one known as the Lost Dutchman Mine.

The mine is supposed to be somewhere in the rugged and hostile Superstition Mountains of Arizona. As the name indicates, the mountains had a bad reputation—even before the stories of the lost mine began.

According to the legend, in the 1840s a Mexican family named Peralta first discovered the rich lode of nearly pure gold. The Peraltas were ambushed by the Apaches, who regarded the Superstition Mountains as sacred ground that should never be disturbed or defiled.

A map, or several maps, showing the location of the mine were passed down through the Peralta family, and copies turned up in the hands of prospectors. The maps proved worthless to everyone who tried to use them, until the mid-1860s. Then a secretive German prospector, Jacob Waltz—called the Dutchman—boasted that he had found the lost Peralta lode.

Many people tried to follow Waltz, and some of them, including his own partner, turned up dead under suspicious circumstances.

After Waltz's own death in 1891 the legend of what was by then called the Lost Dutchman Mine had grown. Julia Thomas, a neighbor and friend of the old prospector, said that before his death he told her where the mine was located, though the description he gave was rather poetic and vague. It certainly didn't help her find the lost mine.

Since then an almost steady stream of treasure hunters have been crawling around the Superstitions looking for the mine. In 1931 a retired government worker named Adolph Ruth got hold of one of the alleged Peralta maps. He struck out toward Weaver's Needle, a spot that had been named by Julia Thomas. A couple prospectors and a rancher helped him set up camp, and after that he was never seen alive again. Later, searchers found his skull, pierced by two bullet holes, in the brush. The remainder of his body turned up a few hundred yards away. Found among his bones was Ruth's notebook, containing cryptic jottings hinting that he had indeed found the mine he had been searching for. The map he is believed to have had in his possession had disappeared.

Since Ruth's death no believable claims have been made that the Lost Dutchman Mine has been located. But every year the hopeful head for the Superstitions. They don't all have maps, but they all have guns.

THE LOST COLONY

In many ways the famous Sir Walter Raleigh was a bungler. He was given a grant by Queen Elizabeth I to establish English colonies in what was then the New World. Raleigh's attempts ended in failure, tragedy, and mystery.

In 1585 Raleigh persuaded some five hundred men to sail to Roanoke Island off the coast of what is now Virginia, with the promise that they would become rich "without toil or labor." The prospective colonists discovered that they were not going to become rich and would have to toil very hard just to stay alive. They also found themselves on very bad terms with the local American Indians, and the survivors returned to England on the first available ship.

In July of 1587 a new batch of colonists arrived at Roanoke. They were different. The group of 150 included 17 women and 6 children. One of the women, Elenora Dare, daughter of John White, the colony's governor, was pregnant. Her daughter, named Virginia Dare, was the first English child born in the New World, and her name at least has passed into legend. Unlike the get-rich-quick crowd that had preceded them, these colonists intended to form a permanent settlement.

The colonists found conditions far worse than they had expected. They decided that Governor White should return to England for more supplies. He was expected to return in a matter of months. But when he got to England he found the country totally absorbed in war with Spain, and it was three years before he was able to return with a relief party.

When Governor White finally set foot on the island again no one was on the shore to greet him. The island was totally uninhabited. The houses the settlers had built had apparently been pulled down and replaced by a stockade. But there was no sign that a battle had taken place.

The settlers had agreed upon a distress signal that Governor White would recognize. If anything happened they would carve a cross in some prominent spot. No cross could be found, but on one tree the letters CRO had been carved, and on another the word CROATOAN.

Croatoan was the name of a nearby island and the Indians who inhabited it. The Indians of Croatoan had been exceptionally friendly to the English colonists in the past, and White hoped that the Roanoke colonists had found refuge among them. But the crew of the ship that brought him refused to take the time to make an extensive search. So White was forced to return to England, and the fate of the Roanoke colonists remains a mystery.

One theory contends that the colonists, despairing that help would never arrive, took the boat that had been left for them and tried to sail back to England, only to be lost at sea. According to another theory the colony was overwhelmed either by an Indian attack or by the Spanish, who had no reason to love the English. The colonists may have tried to move to more hospitable areas near the Chesapeake Bay and were then killed there. Survivors may also have taken refuge with friendly Indians and ultimately become part of their tribe. There are some stories of local Indians numbering white people among their ancestors.

We will never know, for it wasn't until the seventeenth century that the islands were revisited by Europeans, and by that time all evidence of the lost colony had disappeared.

THE NON-RUSTING IRON PILLAR

In front of a mosque in Delhi, India, stands a twenty-three-foot-high, six-ton iron pillar. It was erected in the fourth century and is similar to other iron pillars in the region, except in one respect. This particular metal shaft has shown only the faintest signs of rust, after standing in the open for 1,600 years. For many years the pillar's remarkable durability has excited speculation about unknown technological secrets.

At one time it was believed that the pillar was made of a single piece of metal, a feat that could not have been performed by the most advanced European foundries until the nineteenth century. Now most agree that the pillar was made from a number of smaller iron pieces hammered together while they were still hot.

This technique may account for the pillar's resistance to corrosion. The repeated heating and hammering could have formed a protective coating. Another possibility is that the iron in the pillar has somewhat different composition than modern iron, and that is what gives it its durability. And there are those who believe that the real secret is in the dry, relatively pollution-free atmosphere of Delhi.

In fact, no one really knows for sure.

TOPPLED HEADS

Somewhere around 1150 B.C. a civilization that we call the Olmecs arose in Central America. That was long before the more famous Mayan civilization. The Olmecs may have been the first high civilization in the New World.

They left behind no written language, nor does there seem to be any memory of them in the traditions of later peoples of the region. We don't even know what they called themselves. Fabrics, wood and other delicate items soon decay in the steamy Mexican jungles in which the Olmecs lived. We know them primarily from their sculpture, which has survived. This ranges from small jade statuettes of children with snarling jaguar faces to colossal stone heads, wearing what look very much like football helmets.

The heads are the best-known Olmec remains. Many are six feet high and weigh several tons. The source of the stone for these heads was as much as thirty miles away from where the heads were set up. It would have taken a tremendous amount of time and effort to haul the stones and carve them. They must have meant a lot to the people who had them made. But what did they mean? We haven't the faintest notion. They seem to have been set up as decorations for thrones or altars. They may be the faces of kings or priests or gods. They may even be what they look like—the heads of athletes. The Olmecs would not have been the only society to memorialize celebrated athletes in stone.

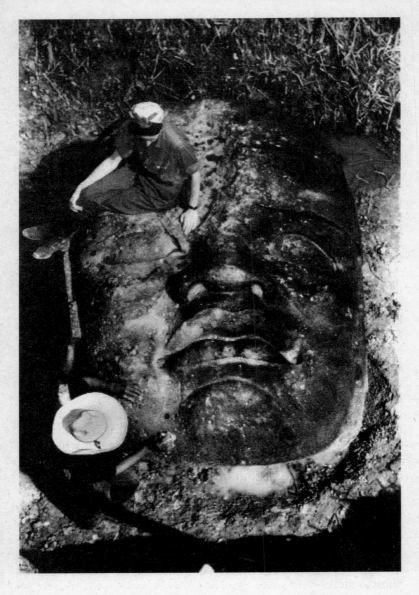

Unearthing one of the great stone heads of the Olmecs.

Since we know so little about them, the Olmecs are, by definition, a mysterious people. But the greatest mystery is what happened to them.

Somewhere around 950 B.C. all the Olmec statues were deliberately broken and defaced. Large pieces were hacked out of the altars. Some sculptures were apparently hoisted high in the air and then dropped on other statues to shatter them both. The great stone heads were tipped over, gouged with symmetrically arranged holes, and then ritually buried in gravel pits.

The destruction appears to be so ritualistic that some have suggested that this was all part of a regular ceremony of destruction and renewal. But since the Olmecs never did recover, invasion or revolt seems a more likely explanation. There is no sign that Olmec lands were taken over by another culture, so that leaves revolt, an overthrowing of the ruling dynasty by the peasants. Yet the destruction was carried out in an orderly and planned manner, rather than in a burst of fury and hatred which is most common in revolution. The fate of the Olmecs remains the greatest mystery of these mysterious people.

WHAT HAPPENED TO THE MAYA?

The Maya are generally considered to have been the greatest of the Indian civilizations of the New World. They were, for example, the only ones to have a written language. It is generally believed today that the European conquest following the discoveries of Columbus destroyed the Mayan civilization. The Europeans did destroy the Incas of Peru and the Aztecs of

Mexico, but by the time they arrived in America, Mayan civilization had nearly disappeared. And no one knows why.

The civilization of the Maya was well established throughout Central America. They built magnificent cities, temples and pyramids. The impressive ruins still attract hordes of awestruck tourists every year. Exquisite Mayan pottery and statuary are the prize possessions of many museums, and these pieces fetch enormous prices when sold on the antiquities market. Scientists are still impressed by the engineering accomplishments of the Maya, who possessed a more accurate calendar than the one used in Europe.

Yet starting around the middle of the fifteenth century, Mayan civilization seemed to fall into a steep decline. The Maya were never a single integrated nation or empire; rather the Mayan world was made up of scattered and often warring city-states. It might seem that if one or two of these independent states collapsed, others would still survive. But one after the other, the Mayan cities fell into decay and ruin; within just a few generations this great and flourishing culture had collapsed. The population was reduced to about one-third of its former numbers.

No shortage of theories exist about what caused the collapse. Some have suggested epidemics, earthquakes, civil war or invasion, but there is no concrete evidence upon which to base any of these theories.

Currently, the most popular theory is that the Maya fell victims to their own success. The more successful they became, the more their population grew, doubling in a century. But soon the soil became exhausted, unable to sustain the demand for more and more crops. As food shortages set in, so did the inevitable decline. More manpower was needed to produce food, and so the number of people available to build and maintain the cities fell. Malnutrition opened the way for disease, and competition for shrinking resources resulted in more warfare. In the end, Mayan culture could not tolerate the strains, and it crumbled.

Since the Maya left no records of what had happened, all of this is only a theory, but it is a plausible one. In our increasingly crowded world, it may contain a lesson for us.

THE GRAVE OF THE CONQUEROR

The Mongol leader Genghis Khan was the greatest conqueror the world has ever known, far surpassing the likes of Alexander the Great and Napoleon. He started life as a fugitive, on the run from his own tribal enemies, and wound up with an empire that ultimately ruled most of Asia and a large part of Eastern Europe. As much as any individual, the great Khan changed the history of the world.

When the Khan died in August of 1227 his body was taken back to his Mongolian homeland and buried in a grave that he had chosen many years earlier. According to Mongol records, the grave was in the shelter of a single tree at the base of Mount Burquan Qaldun in Mongolia's remote Khingan range. It was said that a fabulous royal treasure taken from all the lands the Mongols had conquered was buried with Genghis Khan.

The contents of the conqueror's tomb would not only be priceless, but would be of incalculable historical value as well. The problem is that no one knows where Ghenghis Kahn was buried.

Unlike the Egyptians and others who built elaborate and very obvious tombs for their kings, the Mongols were very secretive. After funeral ceremonies that lasted for months the Mongols did everything they could to obliterate all traces of their leader's burial place. Considering how the pyramids of Egypt and practically every other rich grave site has been plundered, what the Mongols did was probably very wise. And it worked.

兀太祖

铁木眞

No one knows where Genghis Khan, the greatest conqueror the world
has ever known, is buried. (Thames & Hudson, *The Mongols*)

No marker of any sort was placed on the grave. Trees were planted around the lone tree, and eventually any trace of the grave was swallowed up in the forest. Today, the mystery is deeper than ever, for no one even knows which mountain was called Burquan Qaldun in the days of the great Khan.

Several unsuccessful expeditions to find the grave have been mounted, but just poking around Mongolia without any additional information is likely to prove fruitless. One suggestion is that satellite photography might be able to pick up disturbances of the earth and vegetation over the grave site, which would not be noticed on the ground. Another possibility is that a careful review of Mongol records, which have never really been adequately studied, might yield clues as to the location.

And perhaps, just perhaps, there are people in Mongolia today who know the location of the grave. After the burial, certain Mongol clans were given the task of keeping the grave hidden. Even today, many Mongols still revere the memory of the great conqueror. Some believe the secret may have been passed down by word of mouth from generation to generation among a small and select group.

THE FOUNTAIN OF YOUTH

The search for physical immortality is as old as human history. In one of the oldest known works of literature, the ancient Babylonian poem the *Gilgamesh Epic,* the hero Gilgamesh sets out to find a magical plant that will restore his youth. He finds it but then loses it.

For centuries, alchemists searched not only for the secret of turning base metals into gold but also for a substance called the elixir of life, which was supposed to confer immortality or at least a very long life.

One of the most curious searches in history was that of Juan Ponce de León for the legendary Fountain of Youth. As a young man Ponce de León sailed on Christopher Columbus's second voyage to the New World. Later, Ponce de León became governor of Puerto Rico and was one of the most powerful Spaniards in the New World. During his time in the New World he had heard legends of a fountain with magical properties that cured illness and restored youth. The legends were not very specific about where this fountain was located. Some sources seemed to point to the island of Bimini in the Bahamas.

In 1513 Ponce de León was able to mount an expedition to look for the fabled fountain. For some reason he sailed to Florida, which he believed was just another island. There he picked up stories of a sacred spring located in the "country of Tegesta." Ponce de León and his followers plunged through the swamps and jungles of the Florida wilderness, but when they finally found the spring they were looking for they were told that it lost its magical powers or never had them in the first place.

Undiscouraged, Ponce de León pushed on following other rumors. In an abandoned village he found one old man. Ponce de León asked him about the Fountain of Youth, and the old man's reply, roughly translated, was, "If it were here, would I look like this?"

Finally Ponce de León gave up on Florida and headed back to his ships, intending to sail to Bimini. But he missed the island again and wound up on the Yucatán peninsula. There, too, he heard rumors of magical springs. Here the accounts grow fuzzy. According to some he found a spring that he took to be the Fountain of Youth and not only drank from it but took a bottle of the water home for his wife. However, it didn't seem to do him any good. In 1521 he was seriously wounded by a native's arrow, and he asked for the last of the miraculous water to drink. He died anyway at the age of sixty-one.

58

CITY X

Colonel Percy Harrison Fawcett was a loner, an adventurer, a romantic and probably more than a bit of a fraud. He had been a surveyor with the British army and spent years mapping the jungles of Ceylon and South America. He retired from the army in 1925 and started a bizarre quest for what he believed to be a lost city somewhere in the jungles of Brazil.

Fawcett's obsession with finding a lost city began when the adventure novelist H. Rider Haggard, who had often written of lost civilizations in his books, gave the ex-army man a strange-looking, black stone idol inscribed with a mysterious script. Haggard said that the ten-inch statue had been found in Brazil. It all sounded like something out of one of Haggard's stories.

Fawcett's next move was to take the idol to a psychic. He was told that it came from "a large irregularly shaped continent stretching from the north coast of Africa across to South America." To Fawcett that sounded as if the artifact could only have come from the lost continent of Atlantis, and that somewhere in the midst of the Brazilian jungle must exist the remains of an Atlantean colony. The theory that survivors of the sinking Atlantis had brought civilization to South America had been a popular one, though scientists had always scoffed at it.

Fawcett got hold of an old map that showed an unnamed city set deep in the jungle known as Mato Grosso in southwest Brazil. Fawcett called the place City X and somehow convinced himself that this was the Atlantean colony. He set off to find it accompanied only by his son Jack and his son's friend Raleigh Rimell.

Though Fawcett had a good deal of experience with the South American jungle, he and his two young companions were not equipped for an expedition to some unknown point in the middle of the jungle. Fawcett sent back a couple letters to his wife from a Brazilian outpost and wrote about hearing rumors of an ancient city on a lake. And that was the last authentic word that anyone ever heard from Colonel Fawcett.

The environment into which Fawcett plunged was a hostile one, and so were the tribes that lived there. The three could have been killed in many ways, and the chances their bodies would ever be found were slim. But for decades after the disappearance, rumors of travelers encountering a crazed, gaunt, old white man who called himself Fawcett came filtering out of the jungles. So did tales of blue-eyed Indian children supposedly fathered by the adventurers. And there were those who believed that Fawcett actually found his City X and liked it so much he never left.

An Irish medium named Geraldine Cummins said that in 1936 she had received telepathic messages from the adventurer saying that he had found relics of Atlantis in the jungle, but that he was ill and unable to return. Twelve years later the same medium said she received another message from Fawcett informing the world of his own death.

Fawcett's fate remains a mystery; so do his motives for undertaking the foolhardy trip in the first place. Did he really believe that he was going to find an unknown city in the middle of the jungle?

III.
Things

59

CROP CIRCLES

In about 1980, flattened areas of corn or wheat began appearing mysteriously in fields in Britain. These areas were generally circular in shape and could be quite large, up to hundreds of feet in diameter. The flattened areas were produced overnight, and no one saw who or what created them. A field of growing corn that a farmer said was undisturbed when he went to bed would the next day contain one or more circles. "They were," said the British scientist Lord Zuckerman, "creations of the dark." The phenomena were soon dubbed "crop circles."

Reports of similar types of circles or vortexes had appeared from time to time. Back in the seventeenth century a story was told of the "mowing devil," a diabolical creature that mysteriously cut down circular patches of wheat in the fields of Hartfordshire, an area where modern crop circles have been common. Crop circles were also reported as appearing in Australia, Germany and Japan. But the mystery remained essentially a modern British one.

The number of circles seemed to increase year by year, and by 1987 they were becoming more elaborate. Circles appeared within circles and sometimes noncircular patterns appeared in fields. These were given the name pictograms.

As news of the mystery spread, circle spotter groups were formed. Volunteers would conduct all-night vigils, sometimes for weeks, near fields they thought to be likely targets for new circles. After a while the amateur spotters (who sometimes

An elaborate crop circle that appeared in a wheat field in Wiltshire, England. (Wide World photo)

called themselves crop watchers or cerealogists) were joined by television crews, for the crop circles had become big news worldwide. But there were no credible reports of seeing a circle actually being formed. There were, however, frequent reports of strange lights being seen in the areas—UFOs were often mentioned. Some observers said that they felt ill after entering the circles, and others said they could measure electrical changes inside the figures.

Theories as to what might be going on multiplied. Many believed that a previously unknown natural phenomenon was at work—anything from small whirlwinds to troops of badgers madly running around in a circle. Others suggested supernatural forces or suspected that UFOs were somehow involved. One pictogram seemed to spell out the message: WEARENOT-ALONE. And there were those who thought the whole thing was a gigantic hoax.

The biggest hoax news came in September 1991 when two retired artists, Doug Bower and Dave Chorley, claimed that they had been making crop circles in southern England since 1979. A self-styled crop circle expert had declared one of Bower and Chorley's creations to be genuine, something that no human being could have made. When he was told the truth he declared, "We have all been conned."

Even if the hoax claims of Bower and Chorley are true, the two men certainly could not have been responsible for the hundreds and hundreds of circles and pictograms that have appeared over the years, some on the very same night at locations distant from one another. Was there a large team of hoaxers at work, or is there something else involved? The speculation is sure to continue.

THE WITCH CULT

For most people the word *witch* conjures up the image of Margaret Hamilton in *The Wizard of Oz,* an old crone in a black dress and peaked black hat who flies around on a broom. But many today take a more serious view of the subject. There are those who believe that witches are real and part of a powerful worldwide Satanic conspiracy. Others who are equally convinced of the reality of witchcraft believe the witches are the surviving representatives of an ancient religion that worshipped a mother goddess.

The word witch is hard to define. In a general sort of way

it has meant a person, usually a woman, who knows and practices magic, often for evil purposes.

Throughout much of the middle ages Europe was swept with an hysterical fear of witchcraft. Countless people were tortured and executed for allegedly practicing witchcraft and for being in league with the devil. The hysteria even afflicted the American colonies, culminating in the notorious witchcraft trials in Salem, Massachusetts.

By the eighteenth century most educated people had concluded that the whole deadly witchcraft excitement had been a superstitious delusion and that there never had been any witches but merely victims of religious bigotry and greed. The term *witch hunting* became synonymous with looking for a crime that does not exist.

That was the general attitude until the 1920s when a distinguished British anthropologist and Egyptologist, Professor Margaret Murray, wrote a book called *The Witch Cult in Western Europe*. It was Professor Murray's theory that there really had been a large underground cult of witches in Europe, but rather than being devil worshipers, they were pagans, followers of an ancient religion that had been suppressed by Christianity.

According to Professor Murray, the cult had been wiped out. But shortly after the publication of her book a number of people came forward to say that they were members of this ancient and underground cult. Soon, "covens," the name given to gatherings of witches, were springing up all over the British Isles and in America as well. These modern witches called themselves followers of "Wicca," "The Old Religion" or "New Pagans." Some of these groups' members said they had directly inherited the old beliefs; others said they had been able to "reconstruct" the old religion. All said the only sort of magic they practiced helped people and they had nothing whatever to do with Satanism. Satan, they said, was a Christian concept, and their religion predated Christianity.

This collection of beliefs and practices with its emphasis on ecology, feminism and sexual freedom attracted a good deal of attention during the 1960s and 1970s, though just how many

The traditional picture of a witch—an old crone with a peaked hat and a black cat.

followers any of these groups had is difficult to determine. As interest in modern witchcraft grew, so too did opposition. At first these witches were regarded mainly as harmless eccentrics. But many religious groups began to look at them in the same way as ecclesiastics had back in the sixteenth and seventeenth centuries—as part of a vast Satanic conspiracy.

Most historians and scholars do not believe an underground witch cult ever existed in Europe. Some old pagan practices had survived, and people sometimes tried to practice magic, which was forbidden, but nothing was ever organized. Modern witches, say the scholars, are not reconstructing an ancient religion; they are inventing one out of a mishmash of ideas. They certainly possess no magic powers whatsoever. As for the modern witch hunters, though they spread tales of widespread ritual murder, there is simply no evidence to back up the charges.

THE GREAT SIBERIAN EXPLOSION

At 7:17 A.M. on June 30, 1908, something from space slammed into a remote area of Siberia and exploded. The blast created a "pillar of fire," visible for hundreds of miles. The impact was recorded on seismographs throughout the world. A wide range of electrical and magnetic disturbances as well as unusual twilights and sunsets directly attributable to the Siberian blast were recorded for months.

Yet the area was so remote, and conditions so unsettled in Russia at the time, that it wasn't until 1927 that a scientific expedition actually visited the area. On April 13, 1927, the expedition began to see the first signs of the catastrophe. Mile after mile of the ground was covered with burned and broken trees, all pointing in the same direction away from the center of the blast. Approximately one hundred square miles of pine forest had been devastated.

The general expectation was that the Earth had been struck by a large meteorite, and the scientists expected to find a meteorite crater at the center of the devastated area. But there wasn't any crater. Obviously there had been an enormous explosion in 1908, but no large solid object seems to have actually hit the ground. Immediately the meteorite theory lost favor.

Over the years a number of other theories have been offered: The explosion was caused by a meteorite made of antimatter and was totally destroyed by contact with the atmosphere. The culprit was a tiny piece of black hole that went right through the Earth and came out the other side. The explosion was caused by the crash of a nuclear-powered extraterrestrial spaceship. There are other equally farfetched explanations.

The explanation that gained most support among scientists was that Siberia was hit by a piece of a comet. Unlike a meteorite, which is solid, a comet is made up of frozen gases in which small particles of solid matter may be embedded. The comet could have burned up in the atmosphere before reaching the Earth's surface. The passage of the comet through the atmosphere would have generated enough heat to create the pillar of fire that was reported by some witnesses. It would have also produced the shock waves necessary to knock down all the trees and to be felt as much as four hundred miles away.

In January 1993 a scientific team studying the mystery came up with what they said was the most believable explanation— the blast was caused by a stony asteroid one hundred or so feet in diameter. Using computer simulations, the scientists calculated that the asteroid would have exploded and fragmented some five miles above the surface of the earth. The shock waves from the blast would have caused the devastation.

The team concluded that it has "wrapped up" the mystery. But it has been "wrapped up" before. Perhaps we will never

This photo was taken about twenty years after something slammed into the remote Siberian wilderness. The destruction was still clearly visible. (Sovfoto)

know for sure what happened, and that may be a good thing. To be quite sure of what hit Siberia in 1908, the Earth would have to experience a similar event for comparison. Next time, the impact might not be in so remote and unpopulated an area, and the effects could be infinitely more devastating.

ANCIENT ASTRONAUTS

The modern age of flying saucers, also known as unidentified flying objects, or UFOs, began in 1947. But many people who believe that UFOs are really spaceships from other planets say existing evidence proves that Earth was visited by extraterrestrials hundreds, even thousands, of years ago.

UFO believers say that a number of passages in the Bible suggest alien contacts. The most frequently cited is the passage that describes the prophet Ezekiel's vision:

"As I looked, behold, a stormy wind came out of the north, and a great cloud, with brightness round about it, and fire flashing forth continually, and in the midst of the fire, as it were gleaming bronze. And from the midst of it came the likeness of four living creatures. And this was their appearance: they had the form of men, but each had four faces, and each of them had four wings." (Ezekiel 1:4–6)

The description goes on for some length, and it is far from clear what is being described.

The prophet Elijah is said to have ascended into the sky in

a "chariot of fire." Flying chariots also figure prominently in the legends of the Chinese and the people of India.

Figures wearing what appear to be space helmets of some sort are represented in ancient African artwork and in the rock paintings of the Australian Aborigines. What looks to some like a drawing of a man crammed into a space capsule was found in Mayan art. Representations that have been interpreted as spaceships can even be found in medieval art.

By the late 1960s the theory that Earth had been visited not just once but many times in the past by ancient astronauts had developed a large following and was the subject of a number of books, some of them international best-sellers.

Theories of why the extraterrestrials kept coming back to earth without ever actually revealing themselves spanned a wide range. Some believed that the space people appeared only at a time of crisis for the human race—for example, in the late 1940s when we had developed atomic weapons and faced the possibility of exterminating ourselves. Others believed that the space people had brought civilization to the human race. A more extreme view held that we were the product not of earthly evolution but of some kind of extraterrestrial biological experiment.

Critics point out that it's extremely difficult to base any theories on interpretations of ancient legends and art, because so many interpretations are possible. The celebrated drawings of men in space helmets could more easily and logically be seen as drawings of men in ceremonial masks, for example.

Interest in the ancient astronaut theory began to fade when its most influential proponent, Swiss author Erich von Daniken, was conclusively shown to have not only made serious errors in his research, but to have endorsed the authenticity of artifacts that were outright and obvious frauds.

Currently, not a great deal is heard about ancient astronauts, but like all theories of this type, there is always a potential for a sudden rebirth of interest.

ANIMAL MUTILATIONS

From time to time there appear to be waves of unexplained killings and mutilations of animals, usually cattle. During the 1970s, for example, stories of cattle mutilations throughout the Western states created a genuine climate of concern, even fear, among many ranchers and farmers. The stories also generated an enormous amount of publicity.

Rumors blamed the mutilations on members of a satanic cult that practiced animal sacrifice. One psychiatrist warned that the mutilations might be the work of a madman who was likely to switch to human victims.

Even stranger explanations were to come. A few people reported seeing "the Thing," a hairy "man animal" in the region. Though no one said that they saw "the Thing" killing cattle, the connection seemed obvious enough. Bigfoot was roaming the range chewing up livestock.

Most popular was the UFO explanation. At about the time of the mutilation scare were several reports of unidentified flying objects. Somehow, the UFOs and the cattle mutilations became connected in the minds of many. They suspected that alien creatures from UFOs were killing cattle and taking pieces as specimens.

None of this, not even the UFO explanation, was really new. In 1897, when rumors of a "mysterious airship" were rampant in the United States, a Kansas farmer said he had seen the airship, "occupied by six of the strangest beings I ever saw," rope one of his cows and pull it up into the ship. Later, pieces of the butchered animal were found scattered over a neighbor's field. The story was retold countless times and probably still is. However, there is absolutely no doubt it was a hoax. Descendants of the farmer who first told the story recalled how he often laughed at everyone who had taken it so seriously.

During the height of the 1970s scare, special patrols had been organized throughout the affected area in an attempt to catch red-handed the satanic cultists, alien invaders or whatever, at their dirty and deadly business. The patrols never came across anything out of the ordinary.

Veterinarians who examined the remains of the mutilated animals didn't find anything out of the ordinary either. It appeared the animals died of natural causes and the mutilations were caused by small predators chewing away at the carcasses. Dead and partially eaten animals are a common feature of ranch life.

Why the excitement then? No one is really sure. One possible contributing cause is that insurance companies would reimburse ranchers for acts of vandalism but not for deaths resulting from natural causes.

Despite all the cold water that has been thrown on the subject, sensational reports of waves of animal mutilations continue to pop up regularly.

CODE OR HOAX?

In 1822 a handsome stranger calling himself Thomas Jefferson Beale came to the Lynchburg, Virginia, inn run by Robert Morriss. When he departed, he left a locked iron box in the innkeeper's care. A short time later Morriss got a letter from Beale that said if he did not return in ten years Morriss should open the box. The letter also said the box contained papers that could not be understood without "the aid of a key." The key, said the letter, would be furnished later. It never was.

Twenty-three years went by and Morriss decided that it was finally time to open the box. Inside was a long letter with a story about a caché of silver and gold supposedly buried in the foothills of Virginia's Blue Ridge Mountains. The box also contained coded documents that would reveal the exact location of the treasure.

A year before his death Morriss handed Beale's box and its contents over to a friend, James Ward. Ward decided that the cipher's key was the Declaration of Independence, and he was able to crack one part of the Beale code, the part describing the contents of the treasure horde—3,000 pounds of gold, 5,000 pounds of silver and an unknown quantity of precious stones. However, he was not able to decipher the other two documents, one of which gave the location of the treasure.

In 1885 Ward gave up trying and published a pamphlet containing the story and the coded messages. Since that time the Beale Papers have frustrated the finest cryptographers and foiled the most up-to-date computers. There is even a society, the Beale Cipher Association, whose members are devoted to finding the secret of the documents.

That the cipher had defied the most sophisticated analysis has led some to believe that no key exists and the whole thing is an elaborate hoax. There are other reasons for suspicion. The original Beale papers disappeared; indeed, the only evidence that they ever existed is Ward's pamphlet. Beale's writing style has many similarities to Ward's.

Still, there are those who have not only tried to crack the code, but who have dug up parts of the Blue Ridge Mountain foothills trying to find the horde. One treasure hunter said he actually found three empty vaults and is convinced that the Beale treasure is real, but someone already found it.

FIREWALKING

In places such as the Fiji Islands a ceremony is performed in which individuals walk barefoot across a pit filled with red-hot coals. The spectacle has excited wonder and admiration among Western visitors to the island. Whatever its original meaning, the firewalking ceremony was soon converted into a tourist attraction.

As early as 1935, representatives of the British Medical Association went to Fiji to study the firewalkers. The doctors expected to find some sort of stage illusion, but what they saw was a real pit filled with real red-hot volcanic rocks. The Fiji firewalkers danced about on the stones without any sort of protection and without taking any painkillers. Their feet were not burned or blistered by the experience. But there was nothing abnormal or unusual about the firewalkers either. When doctors tested them by putting burning cigarettes to the soles of their feet, the firewalkers reacted in the normal way: They pulled their feet away and later the burned spot blistered. The doctors were impressed and puzzled. The phenomenon was real but they could offer no explanation for it.

In the 1980s firewalking enjoyed a brief popularity in the United States. A man named Tony Robbins taught firewalking as part of a self-mastery technique. His seminar was called "Fear into Power: The Firewalk Experience." Students "graduated" by walking barefoot across a pit with red-hot coals. They could do it, Robbins said, because he had taught them to master their fears. Others also taught firewalking but offered different and sometimes mystical explanations for their technique.

Skeptics said that the secret to firewalking was in the coals. Most firewalkers use volcanic rocks, which are highly porous and poor conductors of heat. Anyone could do it without any special training. All you had to do was step lightly and walk quickly. Hesitate and you get burned. They backed up their beliefs by presenting firewalking demonstrations of their own.

THE DOOMSDAY ROCK

One only has to look at the cratered surface of the moon to realize that bodies in our solar system are struck regularly by large meteorites and other astronomical debris. The Earth, too, has been hit. The so-called Meteor Crater in Arizona is the most obvious evidence of such a collision. Unlike the Moon, which is geologically dead and retains the scars of collisions, most impact craters on Earth have been partly or completely obliterated by erosion and other geological forces. If the Earth were as geologically dead as the Moon, its surface would be as cratered as that of the moon.

Scientists also realize that an unknown but fairly large number of massive chunks of space debris pass within striking distance of the Earth regularly. There was a modest scare in June 1968 when an asteroid called Icarus came within a few million miles of Earth—close in astronomical terms—but not a real threat. Interest in collisions picked up when scientists discovered that the dinosaur extinction may have resulted from Earth's collision with a large asteroid some 65 million years ago. Remains of the impact crater may have been found off the coast of Mexico.

If it happened before, it could happen again, and in recent years scientific interest has been growing in what has been called "the doomsday rock"—an asteroid large enough to severely disrupt life on Earth.

Dr. Tom Gehrels, who heads a scientific team that keeps a

lookout for killer asteroids, was quoted in *The New York Times* as saying: "Eventually it will hit and be catastrophic. . . . The largest near-Earth one we know of is 10 kilometers in diameter (about 6.2 miles). If a thing like that hit, the explosion would be a billion times bigger than Hiroshima. That's a whopper."

In 1990 the U.S. Congress called for detailed studies of the problem. The National Aeronautics and Space Administration has developed a modest program for detecting Earth-crossing asteroids, and a 1991 conference on the subject was well attended.

Scientists are also beginning to look seriously at the possibility of actually blowing up a large asteroid in space before it can hit the Earth, or using an explosion to nudge it into a different and less dangerous path.

Just how likely is collision with a large asteroid? Estimates vary widely from one in 6,000 to one in 20,000 or more, much more. No one really knows.

DOWSING

Probably the most widely used magical or semimagical practice in the world is dowsing, also called divining or witching. Even today in some rural communities in America, the water dowser remains a familiar figure.

Traditionally, the dowser grips a forked stick in his hands and walks to and fro across an area where the stick, apparently of its own volition, moves suddenly. The movement may be up or down, depending on the dowser. The ground below is where water is to be found closer to the surface and thus the best place to dig a well.

Dowsing, though not only for water, goes back a long way. The first real records we have come from a sixteenth-century German book. It was already a well-established practice in Germany at the time. Dowsing spread from Germany throughout Europe and to the United States. Dowsing is practiced widely in Asia and Africa, but whether these traditions developed independently of Europe or came from a single, more ancient tradition is unknown.

In the sixteenth century forked sticks were used most frequently to locate metal ores.

Most of today's water dowsers appear to be honest and sincere people who believe deeply in what they are doing, though they have no explanation as to why the process works. Some will offer a religious explanation, saying that the power can be found in the biblical story where Moses strikes the rock with his rod and water pours forth. A few have more elaborate theories about electromagnetic waves. Some use a scientific-sounding name such as *radiesthesia* to describe the technique.

Critics say that dowsing, assuming the dowser is not a deliberate faker, relies on unconscious and involuntary muscular movements that cause the stick to jump. The dowser is usually familiar with the area in which he is working. Underground water may betray its presence by clues on the earth's surface, such as certain rocks, the color of the soil or the shape of the ground. After years of experience the dowser may have become an expert in recognizing these clues, even though he is not consciously aware of them. Besides, if you drill deep enough, you will find water practically anywhere. A variety of controlled tests with dowsers have yielded results that are at best ambiguous, and the scientific community remains unconvinced that dowsers possess any special powers.

Searching for water with a forked stick is only the most common form of dowsing. Many other objects—from a wire coat hanger to a pendulum—have been used. Some diviners use no rod or pendulum but simply hold their hands out in front of

An illustration of miners dowsing for metal ore taken from an old
book on metallurgy.

them and wait for their muscles to experience a sudden, involuntary, downward pull. Dowsers have looked for metal ores, oil, lost objects, buried treasure, underground pipelines, hidden land mines and even buried bodies.

Some dowsers have claimed that they can locate the objects they are looking for by holding a pendulum over a map.

Despite all the scientific skeptics, thousands of dowsers live in the United States, and millions swear by the practice.

THE DOPPELGANGER

Perhaps you have heard the rumor that everybody has a perfect double somewhere in the world. This sort of belief is extremely ancient and widespread. It is found among many primitive peoples. The first case that we know of comes from the ancient Greek philosopher Aristotle. He tells the tale of a man who felt he could not go outside without meeting himself.

The belief in a personal double was particularly well developed in German folklore, where the phenomenon was given the name *doppelganger*. In German folk belief, the doppelganger was usually a warning of impending death. The subject was used by a large number of writers: Dostoyevsky, Kafka, Oscar Wilde, Edgar Allan Poe and many others. But what is most interesting is that a number of writers reported actually seeing their own doubles.

The most celebrated account was that of the French writer Guy de Maupassant. In 1885 he was working on his masterful horror story, "The Horla." Quite unexpectedly a figure opened the door to his study, walked across the room and sat down in front of him. The figure then began dictating the words of the story to Maupassant.

The writer was astonished. How could this person have gotten into his study? How could he know the very words Maupassant intended to write? Who was he? It was then that he realized that the stranger sitting across from him was no stranger at all

"How They Met Themselves," by the English painter Dante Gabriel Rossetti, illustrates the doppleganger legend. (The Fitzwilliam Museum)

but his exact double. The whole scene disappeared quickly, but it left Maupassant thoroughly shaken.

The great German poet Goethe told of meeting himself on the road while out for a ride. The English poet Percy Bysshe Shelley had a more dramatic encounter. While visiting the Italian city of Pisa he was approached by a figure wearing a long cloak and hood that concealed his face. When the figure was within a few feet of the poet, it raised its hood, revealing Shelley's own face. *"Siete sodisfatto?"* asked the double. "Are you satisfied?"

THE SPHINX

The Sphinx is a mythical creature, half man (or woman) and half lion. It was a popular subject for ancient art, and there are literally thousands of sphinxes from Egypt and Greece.

But to most people the word *sphinx* means only one thing: the Great Sphinx that crouches on the plateau of Gaza near the pyramids in Egypt. This huge monument that towers sixty-six feet above the desert sands is nearly as familiar as the pyramids themselves, and like the pyramids has always excited a sense of wonder and mystery. It was supposed, somehow, to be a repository for all manner of lost ancient wisdom.

The sands often buried the sphinx up to its neck, and visitors would press their ear to its lips to receive words of wisdom. Even in the days of the pharaohs the monument had a magical reputation. When the Great Sphinx was finally cleared of sand,

An early nineteenth century drawing shows the Great Sphinx, the Great Pyramid, and a sarcophagus from the pyramid. (New York Public Library)

a granite tablet containing a strange story was found between its front paws.

It told of a prince who was out hunting and stopped to rest in the shadow of the sphinx. He fell asleep and dreamed that the sphinx promised to make him ruler of Egypt—though several of his brothers had a better claim—if he would clear away the sand. On awakening the prince vowed to do so, and when the stand was cleared, he became King Thutmose IV.

The story is probably pure political propaganda. The new king was trying to shore up his shaky claim with a tale indicating he had been specially chosen by the gods. That was a familiar ploy in the royal politics of ancient Egypt. It is clear that Thutmose IV was appealing to a popular belief in the magical powers of the Great Sphinx.

Conventional archeological wisdom has been that the Great Sphinx was built at the same time as the pyramids of Giza, as sort of an afterthought. Stoneworkers had cut the rock for the pyramids at that spot, and when they were finished, a chunk was left over, so it was sculpted into the Great Sphinx. The head was given the idealized likeness of Chephren, the reigning king.

Recently, however, some archaeologists have come to the conclusion that the Great Sphinx is really far older than the pyramids, and they have no idea whose face is supposed to be on the monster.

THE LOST ARK

In the summer of 1981 the Ark of the Covenant became the most famous lost artifact in the world. The reason was the enormously popular adventure film *Raiders of the Lost Ark.*

The Ark of the Covenant is not a Hollywood creation. It is a box, or chest, in which the ancient Hebrews kept the stone tablets inscribed with the Ten Commandments, given to Moses on Mount Sinai, and other "Tokens of the Covenant," presumably other sacred writings. The Book of Exodus in the Bible describes the ark in elaborate, though somewhat obscure, detail. It was a chest made of acacia wood, about four feet long, two feet wide, and two feet high, and plated with pure gold. It was carried on two gold-plated poles inserted through four rings. The cover was decorated with two gold cherubs with outspread wings.

The ark was to be more than simply a receptacle for sacred objects. It was itself sacred. In Exodus God says of the ark: "It is there that I shall meet you, and from above the cover, between the two cherubim over the Ark of the Tokens, I shall deliver to you all my commands for the Israelites.'' This was the origin of the belief that was central to the 1981 film, that the ark itself possessed supernatural power.

Clearly the ark was central to the worship of the ancient Hebrews and one of the most important religious objects in the history of Judaism. However, at some point it disappeared, perhaps during the conquest of the Kingdom of Israel by the Assyrians during the sixth century B.C. No authentic trace of the Ark of the Covenant has been found since.

Over the centuries many have searched for the ark. Their motives have often been religious. An American explorer, Antonia Futterer, wrote in 1927 that discovery of the ark would ''change the belief of millions of people of all nations for the better; be the greatest blow skeptics ever received; and perhaps the greatest modern proof of the authenticity of Holy Writ.'' Futterer's own expedition was unsuccessful. In 1981 an adventurer named Tom Croster said he had actually found the ark, but his claim turned out to be false. There were suspicions from the start, for the claim was issued right after the success of *Raiders of the Lost Ark,* and Croster had already claimed to have discovered all sorts of other biblical relics.

If any traces of the Ark of the Covenant still exist they are probably in Israel or Jordan, not Egypt as depicted in the film. No area in the world has been more thoroughly combed by archaeologists. However, as the unexpected discovery of the Dead Sea Scrolls showed, the Holy Land may still contain surprises.

THE ILLUMINATI

During the 1960s and 1970s rumors were spread of a mysterious secret society called the Illuminati, which in one way or another seemed to control just about everything.

A small and secretive cult called the *Roshaniya*, "the Illuminated Ones," existed in the medieval Moslem world. Its members believed they were inspired by some sort of divine revelation and by the sixteenth century had gained some power in the mountains of Afghanistan. However, they were ultimately defeated and dispersed by their enemies.

But the Illuminati who inspired the later rumors began in Germany in the late sixteenth century and had no known connection with the earlier Moslem group. The leader of this German group was Adam Weishaupt, a professor of canon law at Ingolstad University. The group claimed to be mystically inspired to free humanity from "tyranny."

The group was definitely a secret society and never a very large one. So many romantic and lurid stories were spread about its members that it is now impossible to determine just what they believed and what they did.

Weishaupt was fired from his job at the university when the society's existence was discovered. The group was quickly suppressed, and Weishaupt fled. That's where the authentic history of the Illuminati ends. After that rumor takes over.

According to some, it was this secret, underground group that was responsible for the French Revolution. It is always easier and sometimes more satisfying to blame a secret society for a momentous historical event than it is to try and understand the complex interplay of forces that cause such an upheaval.

In one version of the lore, the Illuminati were supposed to be a secret inner group of the already secret and sometimes suspect Freemasons. Weishaupt and his friends did join the Masons and attempted to take over some of its lodges, but they were unsuccessful.

Of the many stories told of the Illuminati the most extravagant is that after Weishaupt was driven from Germany in 1776, he came to America, where he took the place of George Washington and changed the course of American history. The one extant picture of Weishaupt shows him looking vaguely (very vaguely) like Washington. To many in Europe, it seemed as if the ideals of the American Revolution were identical to those advocated by the Illuminati.

THE ROSICRUCIANS

At one time practically everyone had seen the newspaper or magazine ads soliciting readers to find out more about a group called the Ancient and Mystical Order of Rosae Crucis (AMORC), or more commonly, the Rosicrucians. The group claimed that it could trace its history back to ancient Egypt and that it possessed all manner of ancient wisdom.

In fact, many groups have called themselves Rosicrucian. The name first appeared in 1614 in an anonymous pamphlet that was passed around the town of Cassel, Germany. The pamphlet said that the secret society had been formed over a hundred years earlier by a wandering sage known only as CRS. Later documents asserted that the name of the sage was Christian Rosae Crucis, or Christian Rosenkreutz; hence the name Rosicrucians. The pamphlet asserted that the members of the society were heirs to all manner of ancient, occult or hidden knowledge.

Over the next year, two other anonymously produced Rosicrucian documents appeared. One of them claimed the mysterious brotherhood had decided to make its existence known because, as predicted, the tomb of its founder, Christian Rosenkreutz, had miraculously opened after 120 years.

The original Rosicrucian documents stated that membership in the society was open to all worthy men. If these men would make their interest known, they would be contacted. As far as can be determined no one was ever contacted.

Aside from the pamphlets themselves, no evidence proves the existence of Christian Rosenkreutz or any Rosicrucian Society. The best guess is that the Rosicrucian pamphlets were written by a group of university students led by a man named Johann Andrea. Andrea was interested in mysticism, alchemy and magic. A rose and a cross formed part of his family coat of arms, and in fact Rosicrucians have been called the Brotherhood of the Rose Cross. Andrea actually admitted to composing one of the mysterious documents. If he was indeed the author, his motives are unknown.

In the following centuries the name Rosicrucian was applied to many groups. The term became so popular that it has been used as a description for practically any brand of occult knowledge.

Despite its claims to great antiquity, the familiar AMORC group was actually formed in 1916 by H. Spencer Lewis, an American advertising man with an interest in the occult.

Rosicrucian groups have frequently squabbled among themselves, each claiming to be the true heir to the ancient wisdom. Though they all claim to be secret, disenchanted members are forever revealing the secrets. These generally turn out to be disappointing rehashes of occult rituals or methods of card reading and crystal gazing.

Some still insist that despite all the fraudulent claims and counterclaims a small number of "real" Rosicrucians do possess the ancient secrets. The trouble is, there appears to be no way of identifying these "real" Rosicrucians.

SPONTANEOUS HUMAN COMBUSTION

The belief that people can suddenly, and for no obvious reason, burst into flames and be consumed was exceedingly popular in the nineteenth century. Though scientists universally consider the idea absurd, many still believe in the possibility today.

Spontaneous human combustion has been used in novels by some very famous writers. Both Mark Twain and Herman Melville wrote about drunks who suddenly burned up. There once was a theory that this could happen to people who drank too much.

The most famous case of spontaneous human combustion in literature appears in Charles Dickens's *Bleak House*. The victim is a drunken and miserly rag-and-bone man named Krook, who is instantly reduced to a pile of ashes. Dickens really believed what he wrote, and when criticized for it he defended himself with such vigor that critics were puzzled.

Sensational newspapers of the Victorian era often carried what they said were authentic cases of spontaneous human com-

The most famous case of spontaneous human combustion to occur in literature is illustrated in Charles Dickens's *Bleak House*. (New York Public Library)

bustion, but those papers were about as reliable as supermarket tabloids are today.

During the early 1980s interest was revived in the subject. A number of apparently impressive cases in which people were consumed by fire, while most of their surroundings were left undamaged, were cited.

The conventional explanation in these cases is that the cause of the fire was cigarette smoking, and that the victim was often old and disabled or drunk, and therefore unable to respond quickly once the fire started.

Those who reject the conventional explanation offer others, from poltergeists to unknown forces consciously released by the victim. Perhaps the most bizarre explanation was that some sort of strange "fire beings which swoop down on certain individuals and incinerate them mysteriously" exist.

ANCIENT MAP OF THE ANTARCTIC

In 1929 what appears to be a centuries-old map was found in the Topkapi Palace in Istanbul. The map was supposed to have been drawn in 1513 under the direction of a Turkish admiral (or pirate) named Piri Re'is (Admiral Piri). It shows the Atlantic Ocean and its islands and bordering lands. It also might possibly show the continent of Antarctica before it was covered by its present ice sheet.

The map, which was apparently made a mere twenty-one years after Columbus's voyage, was claimed by the Turks to be the most accurate of the early maps of the New World. Even more intriguing was the statement in one of the inscriptions that the map was based on one that Columbus had used on his first voyage.

There had long been speculation that Columbus possessed a map of the coast of the New World before he set out on his voyage. Such a map would obviously have indicated pre-Columbian voyages. Columbus never said anything about it, and no evidence of such a map has ever been found.

Moreover, another inscription quotes Piri Re'is as saying that he consulted twenty older maps, some dating back to the time of Alexander the Great, in preparing his map. Istanbul was formerly Constantinople, one of the great cities of the ancient world, and it certainly might have been a storehouse for maps and documents from earlier times.

The Piri Re'is map was a short-lived sensation. It was then forgotten until 1956 when it caught the attention of Captain Arlington H. Mallery, a retired navy officer and avid student of old maps. Mallary noticed that on the map the southern tip of South America appears to blend into a large southerly land mass that looked vaguely like the continent of Antarctica. That continent was unknown to the world until the 1820s. Mallery made what he thought was an even more sensational discovery. The map appeared to show a part of the Antarctic coast as it looked before it was covered by a thick ice sheet. The outlines of this area had been traced by a series of expeditions using seismographic equipment in the late 1940s and early 1950s.

Mallery suggested that the Turkish map had been based on information gathered at a time before the ice sheet covered the continent some ten thousand years ago. On the basis of this, Professor Charles H. Hapgood proposed that an ancient civilization of seafarers existed during a warm period between major ice ages. This civilization, said Professor Hapgood, possessed a technology that far surpassed anything known until modern times. It was from information gathered by these ancient sea kings, as he called them, that Piri Re'is had obtained his picture of Antarctica.

A few scholars have admitted the possibility that Bronze Age seafarers from the Mediterranean, trading along the coasts of Africa, may have ventured much farther south than previously believed. However, the notion of an ancient super civilization not only reaching Antarctica but accurately mapping it seems too farfetched.

This raises the possibility that the Piri Re'is map is a sixteenth-century forgery, produced during a period of intense Turkish nationalism, in order to raise the status of Turkey in the eyes of the world.

The forgers would certainly have known the outlines of the coasts of North America and South America. But how would they have known the outlines of Antarctica under the ice sheet? Maybe they didn't. Speculation about a southern continent goes all the way back to the ancient Greeks. The forgers may just have thrown it in. Other mapmakers did. The outlines are very general, and the correlations with pre-ice Antarctica may be coincidental.

But if the map is not a forgery we may have to radically alter our current beliefs about the development of civilization.

THE *MARY CELESTE*

Of all the mysterious disappearances at sea none is more puzzling than the case of the *Mary Celeste*. In November 1872 the brig *Mary Celeste* was docked in New York Harbor while being loaded with a cargo of commercial alcohol, bound for Genoa, Italy. The British ship *Dei Gratia* was also being loaded for a transatlantic voyage at a nearby pier.

The crew of *Dei Gratia* sights the abandoned *Mary Celeste.*

Benjamin Spooner Briggs, captain of the *Mary Celeste,* and David Reed Morehouse, captain of the *Dei Gratia,* were old friends. They had dinner together on the evening of November 3. Two days later the *Mary Celeste* set sail. The *Dei Gratia* got underway on November 11.

On December 5, Captain Morehouse received a nasty shock when he encountered the *Mary Celeste* abandoned and drifting off the coast of Portugal. There was no obvious reason why the ship should have been abandoned. Though her sails were torn, and she was a bit battered, she was completely seaworthy. Members of the *Dei Gratia* crew proved that by sailing her to port in Gibraltar. The *Mary Celeste*'s lifeboat and some of her navigation instruments were missing, but otherwise everything, including the captain's log and all of the crew's gear, was still on board.

The log gave no hint of trouble. At the time of the last entry the ship had been "about 110 miles due west of the island of Santa Maria in the Azores." If the *Mary Celeste* had been abandoned shortly after that entry was made, she must have been empty for over a week and drifted nearly six hundred miles.

As soon as the *Mary Celeste* reached Gibraltar, the authorities began an investigation. A search was made for the missing occupants, but no trace of them was ever found. At first, Captain Morehouse was suspected of having something to do with the disappearance, because by the law of salvage he could claim a substantial profit from having brought in an abandoned ship. No evidence connecting anyone on the *Dei Gratia* to the disappearance was ever presented.

All of the usual reasons for abandoning a ship—storms, pirate attack, mutiny—were considered and discarded. Any of these would have left evidence of damage or struggle, and there was none. In the end the investigators concluded they didn't know what happened.

Since then a host of other explanations have been offered. They range from the suggestion that the crew ate food contaminated with a fungus that drove them to madness and suicide, to the theory that they were plucked from the ship by a passing UFO.

A more probable explanation is that there was a minor explosion among the alcohol casks in the cargo hold. The explosion did no great damage, but it frightened the captain and crew into making for the lifeboat. The lifeboat was then swamped by a wave before it could get back to the undamaged ship.

A reasonable explanation, but an unprovable one.

THE MUMMY'S CURSE

The 1922 discovery of the virtually intact tomb of King Tutank-hamen of Egypt ranks as the greatest archaeological find of the twentieth century. It was certainly the most well publicized.

The discovery is credited to two men, archaeologist Howard Carter and wealthy nobleman Lord Carnarvon, who had financed Carter's work. The story of the curse really began in March 1923, when Carnarvon fell ill and was taken to a Cairo hospital, where he died on April 5. The exact cause of his death is not really known, but it seemed to have been the result of an infection spread from an insect bite. Carnarvon was only fifty-seven. His death was unexpected, and its trivial cause seemed incredible and unnatural.

It is said that a brief power failure occurred in Cairo, at the exact moment of Carnarvon's death, and all the lights went out. Back in England on the Carnarvon estate, one of his favorite dogs began to howl and then mysteriously fell over dead.

Lord Carnarvon's death created very nearly as much a sensation as the original discovery of the tomb. The story of King Tut's Curse, or the Mummy's Curse, was now well launched, and every time someone connected with the discovery died, the rumor went around that the curse had struck again. By 1929 eleven people associated with the discovery had died, including Lady Elizabeth Carnarvon, who improbably enough also died from an infected insect bite.

Carter's personal secretary, Richard Bethell, was found dead

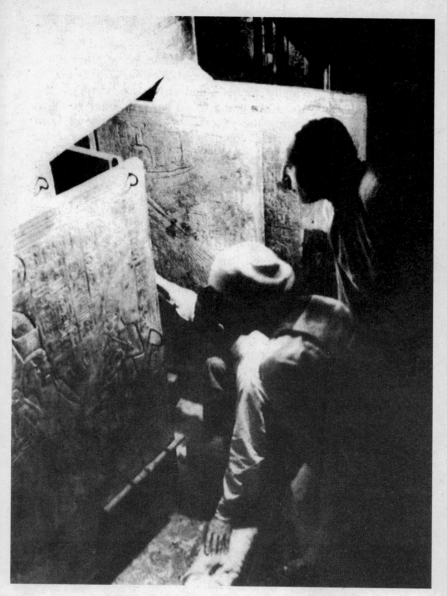

The shrine that held the mummy of King Tut is opened.

in his chair at his London club. The cause of death was never determined or at least never made public. A short time later, Bethell's father, Lord Westbury, jumped to his death from a building near Buckingham Palace. Lord Westbury left behind a note that read: "I really cannot stand any more horrors and I hardly see what good I am going to do here, so I am going to make my exit." During the funeral the hearse carrying Lord Westbury's body knocked down and killed an eight-year-old boy.

In the years that followed, still more deaths were attributed to the curse. By 1935 the number of supposed victims had reached twenty-one.

Most stories of the curse say that an inscription reading "Death shall come on swift wings to him who disturbs the peace of the king" was found somewhere in the tomb. No such inscription was ever found, and Egyptian kings were never known to place curses on those who disturbed their tombs. Royal tombs were regularly disturbed; indeed Tutankhamen's tomb was the only undisturbed royal tomb to be found in modern times. Rumors of curses never frightened tomb robbers.

One archaeologist said that if Egyptian tombs were cursed, then all archaeologists would be dead. The archaeologist Howard Carter, who was the man who really discovered the tomb, never believed in a curse. The mere mention of the subject infuriated him. Carter himself lived until 1939, dying of entirely natural causes at the respectable age of sixty-six. If there had been any curse, death did not come on "swift wings." It waited seventeen years for Carter.

CURSE OF THE HOPE DIAMOND

What was to become the Hope diamond first made its appearance in the seventeenth century when a French trader brought a large, blue diamond from India. It was said that the diamond had been stolen from the eye of an idol and a curse was placed on it.

The diamond was sold to King Louis XIV, who had it cut into a heart shape. At that time it was called the French Blue. The curse, if there was one, didn't trouble Louis XIV, for he was France's most powerful and longest-reigning monarch. The diamond passed down through the royal family to Louis XVI, who gave it to his queen, Marie Antoinette. King and queen lost both their thrones and heads during the French Revolution.

During the revolution the diamond disappeared. Part of it reappeared rather mysteriously in London. It was purchased by banker Thomas Henry Hope, who gave the gem the name by which it is now known.

Hope himself never seems to have been afflicted by any particular ill fortune. After his death the diamond passed to other members of the family. One of those who wore the diamond was May Yohe, a singer who married and later divorced Lord Francis Hope. She died in poverty in 1938, and always blamed the diamond for her ill luck.

But by that time the diamond had long passed out of the Hope family. It was sold in 1901 to a jeweler who went bankrupt. It was then owned by a dissolute Russian nobleman who shot his showgirl lover and who was later stabbed to death by a group of revolutionaries.

The next owner was a Greek jeweler who fell off a cliff. The diamond then turned up in the collection of Sultan Abdul Hamid of Turkey. For good reasons he was called "Abdul the Damned." He went mad and was deposed. The Hope diamond passed through several hands after that until it was sold to Edward B. McLean, heir to a newspaper fortune, and his independently wealthy wife, Evalyn.

It was with the McLean family that the idea of a curse was really solidified. Shortly after purchasing the diamond, McLean's mother died; so did two of the servants in the McLean household. Evalyn McLean was unimpressed. She often wore the diamond, now set in a necklace.

By far the most tragic and extraordinary death in the McLean family was that of ten-year-old Vinson. He had always been watched with unusual care, but one day he slipped away from the servants, ran out in front of the family home in Washington, D.C., and was instantly struck and killed by a car.

The McLean marriage ended in divorce, and heavy drinker Edward McLean wound up in a mental institution where he died.

In 1946 the McLeans' only daughter died as the result of an overdose of sleeping pills. The newspapers recalled that at her wedding five years earlier she had worn the Hope diamond. Evalyn McLean herself died a year later. To the end she firmly rejected any belief in a curse.

The next owner was the famous jeweler Harry Winston, who donated the diamond to the Smithsonian Institution, where today it is still one of the most popular exhibits.

Winston took the unusual step of sending the diamond to the Smithsonian by ordinary parcel post. He paid about $150 for insurance on the package, but otherwise took no extra precautions. The package arrived safely. However, it has been suggested that the diamond put a curse on the U.S Postal Service, from which it has never recovered.

Evalyn Walsh McLean wearing the Hope Diamond. (UPI photo)

AN ANCIENT COMPUTER

One of the most frequently raised criticisms of the ancient Greeks is that while they were great at constructing theories, they were not very practical about making things. But they may have been better than we think.

In 1900 divers located the wreck of an ancient Greek ship off the island of Antikýthēra. Archaeologists determined that the wreck was that of a commercial vessel, sunk about 65 B.C. while on its way to Rome. The cargo was mainly pieces of sculpture, but from the wreckage divers pulled what appeared to be a badly corroded piece of machinery.

The object remained merely a curiosity for years until it was carefully studied by the highly respected academician and historian of science, Professor Dereck de Solla Price. Professor Price decided that the device, which had been made with bronze plates and complicated gears, had been designed to display the positions of the Sun and Moon and possibly the planets. According to astronomer Colin Ronan, "It was an instrument that gave the positions of celestial bodies in figures—there were pointers that moved over dials to indicate the results of its internal calculations. . . . In short, this was a mechanical computer and a complex one at that. Internal evidence also shows that it was a contemporary machine definitely made for everyday use and not a treasure from some bygone age. We are forced to the conclusion that it pays tribute to a tradition of highly advanced technology in Greece. . . . But if there was a tradition of an advanced technology in the ancient world, it did not penetrate into Western Christendom.''

At a scientific meeting, Professor Price told his colleagues, ''Finding a thing like this is like finding a jet plane in the tomb of King Tutankhamen.''

This astronomical ''calculator'' does indicate that the ancients were far more technologically advanced than we have given them credit for. Still, such a device could have been constructed by the extremely clever application of some relatively simple principles that were known to the Greeks and Romans. What is exceptionally interesting about this discovery is that it was completely unexpected. We have fairly voluminous records from this period in history, yet none of them mentions this apparently common device. It was found by accident, and one wonders what other technological marvels may one day turn up in an ancient wreck or undiscovered tomb.

THE VINELAND MAP

On Columbus Day, 1965, Yale University announced, with considerable fanfare, that they had a medieval map, which proved conclusively that the Viking Leif Eriksson had reached North America well before Columbus. The announcement absolutely outraged Italian-American groups, who considered it a direct slap in the face of the great mariner. Yale insisted, not very convincingly, that the timing of the announcement was pure coincidence.

In fact, few scholars doubted that the Vikings had indeed

reached Vineland—what the Vikings called North America—at least four hundred years before Columbus. But scholars believed no extensive or permanent settlement resulted from the contact. Nor did they agree as to exactly where the Vikings landed.

The map was said to have been made by a Swiss monk in around 1440, but he was supposed to have used much older maps as a source. The map contained a remarkably accurate depiction of Europe and Greenland, which the Vikings were known to have colonized, and an island labeled *Vinilanda Insula*—clearly the coast of North America. An inscription mentioned Leif Eriksson.

The map was bound in a manuscript called *The Tartar Relation,* a thirteenth-century account of a Central Asian journey. The documents had been purchased from a European dealer, and their origins were unclear.

The map provided no new information about the Viking voyages to Vineland, but it was dramatic confirmation that the voyages had taken place and indicated that the Viking knowledge of geography was better than had previously been believed.

Despite the prestige of Yale University, the map's sponsor, there were doubters from the start. The map looked too accurate, too modern. Within a few years the wheel had turned. In 1974 other scholars examined the map and found that its ink contained traces of a material that had not been developed until the 1920s. They even believed they found the map from which the forger had made his copy.

Then the wheel turned again, at least part way. In 1985 scientists at the University of California subjected the map to rigorous tests and decided that "the prior interpretation that the map has been shown to be a twentieth-century forgery must be reevaluated."

They didn't come out and say that the map was the genuine article, but they left the door open.

THE KENSINGTON STONE

In 1898 a Swedish-born farmer named Olof Ohman said that he had dug up an inscribed stone on his farm near the village of Kensington, Minnesota. The inscription appeared to be in runes, the alphabetic characters of Northern Europe during the Middle Ages. Translated, the runes told the story of an inland expedition of Vikings during the twelfth century.

That the Vikings had reached the shores of North America during the eleventh century was considered a distinct possibility in the late nineteenth century. Today it is an accepted fact. That the Vikings had journeyed inland as far as Minnesota, which was the home of many modern Scandinavian immigrants, including farmer Ohman, seemed remarkable, almost too good to be true. And when experts looked at the stone they almost unanimously declared that it was too good to be true—the stone was a modern fake, and a crude one at that. Suspicious glances were cast at Ohman, and in embarrassment he took the stone home where he used it as a stepping-stone.

That probably would have been that if the stone had not come to the attention of a Norwegian-American college student named Hjalmar Holland. No cause could ask for a more devoted supporter than Holland. For the rest of his long life Holland championed the Kensington Stone with unflagging energy and remarkable ingenuity. He wrote millions of words on the subject and developed grand theories of a Viking "crusade" to America, based on the evidence of the stone. In 1948, primarily due to Holland's efforts, the Kensington Stone was actually placed on display in the near sacred halls of the Smithsonian Institution in Washington, D.C. Alexandria, Minnesota dedicated a Runestone Memorial Park, featuring a huge replica of the stone.

Holland managed to win a few scholars over to the opinion that the stone was genuine, but the vast majority continued to insist it was a fake. If the stone was a fake, who could have been the faker? Stone supporters always insisted that Ohman was an uneducated man, incapable of producing even a crude forgery. But as the events surrounding the finding of the stone were examined more closely, that picture proved inaccurate. Ohman was considerably more learned than he liked to let on, and with the aid of a schoolteacher friend, he could easily have produced a forged rune stone.

Today, the Kensington Stone controversy isn't as heated as it was when Holland was still alive. Additional knowledge of Viking contacts with North America have not provided any evidence that they ranged as far as Minnesota. But the stone is still defended as a source of ethnic pride by many Scandinavian-Americans. And its influence can still be seen in the name of a professional football team—The Minnesota Vikings.

THE EMERALD TABLET

To many a medieval alchemist and scholar, the most mysterious and valuable document in the world was the Emerald Tablet. According to tradition, the tablet was found in a cave. The words were etched in Phoenician characters on a slab of emerald clutched in the hands of the corpse of Hermes Trismegistus, the legendary founder of alchemy. The discoverer in one version of the story was Sara, the wife of Abraham, and the cave was located near Hebron in what is now Israel. In other versions, the tablet was found by Alexander the Great in the hands of celebrated ancient magician Apollonius of Tyana. Still another variation of the legend had Hermes himself give the tablet to Miriam, the beautiful sister of Moses. In Arabic legend Noah took the Emerald Tablet with him on his ark.

It is clear that considerable importance was attached to the document. But it is not at all clear what it means. The opening lines will give you the flavor of the Emerald Tablet:

> *True it is, without falsehood, certain and most true. That which is above is like that which is below, and that which is below is like to that which is above, to accomplish the miracles of one thing.*
>
> *And as all things were by the contemplation of one, so all things arose from this one thing by a single act of adaption.*
>
> *The father thereof is the Sun, the mother is the Moon.*
>
> *The wind carried in its womb, the Earth is nurse thereof.*
>
> *It is the father of all works of wonder throughout the whole world.*
>
> *The power thereof is perfect.*

It goes on in the same vein for another fifteen or so lines. Aside from expressing a general belief that all Heavenly and Earthly events are connected, and that everything in Heaven and Earth had a single origin, it's difficult to see what the point of it all is. Attempts to explain the Emerald Tablet are usually as obscure as what is contained in the original, and much longer.

A whole body of literature was attributed to Hermes Trismegistus and was supposed to have originated in Egypt and be incredibly ancient. However, historical research has shown that this "Hermetic literature" was mostly composed in Alexandria,

Egypt, during the first few centuries of the Christian era. The authors belonged to a variety of Christian sects that flourished at the time. These sects incorporated ancient magical lore and Greek philosophy into their doctrines. One thing that most impressed medieval scholars is that the documents, which were supposed to be pre-Christian, contained many references to Christianity. They seemed to anticipate the birth of Christianity. However, since they were really written after Christianity was well established, their prophetic nature is less impressive.

The Emerald Tablet may be older than other Hermetic writings, though we cannot be sure. Its first known account appears in a book written in Arabic during the ninth century. Scholars believe that the origin of the document was Greece or Syria, rather than Egypt. The real author is, and doubtless always will, remain unknown.

THE GRIMOIRES

We all carry in our mind's eye the picture of the magician's secret book. The robed sorcerer opens the gigantic book and begins to read aloud—a strange chant in an unknown language. Lightning flashes, thunder cracks and demons rise from the bowels of the Earth. It is a scene reinforced by countless books and movies.

In fact, such secret books existed in the Middle Ages. They were called *grimoires,* a word that comes from the same root as grammar, or "gramayre," an old term for magic and enchantment. Most of the grimoires that survive to the present

A magician summoning a demon with the aid of a grimoire or magic book.

day are not particularly ancient. They were composed in Europe between the sixteenth and eighteenth centuries, although they were based on older material. The authors of the grimoires are unknown, and the books are usually falsely attributed to some celebrated historical or legendary character. The most influential and one of the oldest of these books, *The Key of Solomon,* was supposed to have been written by the biblical King Solomon. The book was compiled sometime between the thirteenth and fifteenth centuries and had nothing whatever to do with King Solomon. Another popular grimoire was attributed to Honorius the Great, an early pope.

The spells in the grimoires are supposed to allow magicians to control the forces of nature or to compel spirits or demons to do their bidding. The magicians believed they could control the demons without the demons gaining any control over them, and most magicians regarded themselves as good Christians. The church held quite a different view; the practice of magic itself was evil, and all who engaged in it were servants of the devil, whether they knew it or not. Sometimes magicians were tolerated, at other times executed.

Most of the spells in the grimoires are unbelievably long and complicated, and it would seem virtually impossible to perform them correctly. Moreover, the magician had to be properly prepared, usually by days or weeks of fasting and abstinence, and even then he had to be in the proper state of mind; his motives for performing the act had to be the right ones and often he had be descended from the right family. No one could perform magic simply by mumbling a few words out of a book.

But the most important thing to know about the grimoires is, despite their powerful reputation, the spells contained in them just don't work. Medieval magicians were usually pathetic figures, who were either hated and feared or simply dismissed as frauds. They moved from place to place, often a step ahead of the authorities and their creditors. Their customers were people more deluded and pathetic than they were, and no single instance of a magician becoming rich or powerful as a result of his practices can be verified.

Still, there was a market for grimoires, and publishers churned them out in great quantity. Far from being secret books, they were available to anyone who had the money to buy one.

ANIMALS AND EARTHQUAKES

Earthquake prediction remains, at best, an uncertain science. But for centuries folk wisdom has held that particular sorts of animals appear to sense an impending earthquake long before humans or their sophisticated scientific apparatus become aware of it.

A 1908 article noted, "In connection with the fearful catastrophes of recent date in Italy, California and elsewhere, which like so many others of like nature, will long retain a hold on human memory, attention has again been called to the fact that many animals give intimations of such great disturbances in advance, by certain particular and often unusual conduct. It is particularly such animals as have their abode underground that often indicate, days before the event, that something unusual in nature is about to occur, by coming out of their hiding places underground into the open."

During the 1930s scientists in earthquake-prone Japan studied catfish in an aquarium. When there was no impending quake the catfish were their usual lazy selves. But about six hours before an earthquake shock they began jumping and swimming around. According to a description of the observations, "Several months' testing showed that in a period when 178 earthquakes of all degrees of severity had been recorded, the fish had correctly predicted 80 percent of the shocks."

In China, which has also suffered greatly from earthquakes, interviews with local people who had survived a major quake produced thousands of accounts of unusual animal behavior shortly before the earthquake. "Some examples included dogs that picked up their offspring and carried them outdoors, pigs that squealed strangely, startled chickens that dashed out of coops in the middle of the night, rats that left their nests, and fish that dashed about aimlessly."

All of this and much more falls into the realm of anecdotal evidence. It is interesting, but it does not constitute scientific proof. And most of the scientists who study earthquakes remain skeptical of such stories. Yet the theory that animals may be able to sense subtle changes before an earthquake is not an entirely implausible one. We do know that earthquakes are sometimes heralded by changes in the magnetic field or sounds that are not within the human range of hearing. Many animals are more sensitive to magnetic fields and sounds than we are. They may be able to detect other changes as well.

EARTHQUAKE WEATHER

People who live in earthquake-prone regions sometimes speak ominously of "earthquake weather," a certain type of atmospheric condition that precedes a major quake.

A nineteenth-century English writer, Richard A. Proctor, provided this rather charming description:

"You are sitting in the piazza, about afternoon teatime let us say, tropical languor, when gradually a sort of faintness comes over the air, the sky begins to assume a lurid look,

the street dogs leave off howling hideously in concert for a minute and even grim vultures perched upon the house-tops forget their obtrusive personal differences in a common sense of general uneasiness. There is an ominous hush in the air, with a corresponding lull in conversation for a few seconds, and then somebody says with a yawn, 'It feels very much like earthquake weather.' Next minute you notice the piazza gently raised from its underpropping woodwork by some unseen force.''

Do certain types of weather conditions occur just before a major earthquake—like this one that devastated Chile in 1960? (The American Red Cross)

William R. Corliss, one of the most diligent collectors of strange events, notes in his *Handbook of Unusual Natural Phenomena:* "Beyond this appealing subjective account lies considerable testimony that the more cataclysmic quakes are presaged and accompanied by fogs, mists, darkness and general obscurations of the atmosphere."

The most frequently mentioned "weather" preceding an earthquake is a sudden feeling of oppressive heaviness, the feeling one often gets before a severe thunderstorm. But there is no satisfactory evidence that any change in barometric pressure precedes a major quake.

"Earthquake weather" may simply be folklore, or it may be the result of some subtle but as yet unexplained change in the atmosphere that affects the perceptions of humans and quite possibly animals.

WITHOUT WHEELS

The discovery of the wheel is generally considered to be one of the most important inventions in human history. From the wheelbarrow to the oxcart and war chariot, the wheel allowed people to move heavy loads at a greater speed. It is not known where or when the first wheel was invented, but by about 1000 B.C. wheeled vehicles were used throughout much of Asia, Africa and Europe. Strangely, the wheel was never used by the Incas, Aztecs or other high civilizations of the New World—though they were technologically advanced in many other areas.

When the Spanish invaded the New World, they found people

who apparently had no independent knowledge of the wheel, and this may, in part, have made them easy prey for invaders from Europe, who in many other respects did not have a technology that far advanced over the native civilizations.

The Incas built a road system as good or better than that of the ancient Romans, and certainly a lot better than anything being built in Europe at the time of the conquest. Yet this magnificent system was used entirely by men on foot or by draft animals carrying relatively small loads on their backs.

There was much speculation as to why the high civilizations of South America and Central America never invented the wheel. One theory was that they had no large draft animals such as horses or oxen to pull carts. The main draft animal was the llama, an animal that, like its close relative, the camel, does not take well to pulling carts. The mountainous terrain through which the Inca roads run would also make wheeled vehicles less useful. On the other hand, lack of suitable draft animals should not have stood in the way of the extremely useful wheelbarrow and handcart. The mountains should not have interfered with the development of the pottery wheel or the spinning wheel. All the South American and Central American Indians were expert textile and pottery makers.

The unsatisfactory conclusion was that for some reason the American Indian civilizations had simply not invented the wheel. Then, in the 1940s, it was discovered that they had invented the wheel! Small representations of animals on wheels turned up at grave sites in Mexico. The wheels were completely functional, and the objects look a lot like pull toys still popular with children today, though we do not know what significance the objects had to the people who made them.

It now appears that the people of the New World had invented the wheel, but for some unknown reason, had made no practical use of it.

LEVITATION

Throughout history tales have been told of individuals, usually holy men, who had the ability to levitate—that is, rise off the ground at will and perhaps fly around. In the East so many tales existed that the ability was regarded as commonplace. There is a story that the Buddha was approached by a would-be disciple, who, to prove his worthiness, levitated and circled the room several times. The Buddha was not impressed. He told his other disciples that they should not be distracted by such performances, but should turn their attention to the more important matter of inner spiritual development.

In the West many tales are told of levitating magicians and saints, but they are so vague that they must be classified as folklore. However, the feats of levitation attributed to St. Joseph of Copertino, a seventeenth-century Italian monk, are somewhat more substantial. Joseph, according to these accounts, was a rather simple ascetic who often fell into trances. Sometimes while in these mystic states his body rose from the ground. There are a number of eyewitness accounts of these feats, though it is impossible to know how reliable the accounts really are.

In the nineteenth and twentieth centuries, levitations became a fairly familiar part of many spiritualist séances. The greatest of the nineteenth-century mediums, the Scotsman D.D. Home, was reported to have floated out one window and in through another in the presence of several witnesses. Unfortunately, the

The nineteenth century medium D.D. Home was said to be able to levitate during séances. (New York Public Library)

accounts of his levitations contain many gaps and inconsistencies, and while they are often cited as the best evidence for the levitation of mediums, they are badly flawed evidence.

Several photographs show mediums allegedly levitating during séances, but they are not at all convincing. In most, the mediums seem quite clearly to be jumping rather than floating.

In 1977 the popular transcendental meditation (TM) movement founded by the Maharishi Mahesh Yogi claimed that its followers could be taught to levitate. However, public demonstrations of TM levitation showed that while people could be taught to hop from a cross-legged position, they were not floating. The hopping was an impressive athletic feat, but it did not violate any known physical laws.

THE INDIAN ROPE TRICK

Of all the magical feats of the "mysterious East" the most fabled is the Indian rope trick. This trick has many versions, and this is the most spectacular:

The magician takes a wooden ball to which a thick piece of rope is attached. He whirls the ball around and releases it high into the air, where it seems to disappear, and does not fall back to earth. The rope attached to it goes straight up, and the upper end of the rope also seems to disappear.

The magician orders his young assistant to climb the rope. At first the boy refuses, but the magician becomes angry, so slowly and reluctantly the boy climbs until he too vanishes.

For a while nothing happens, and the magician becomes restless and angry. He pulls at the rope, but the boy does not reappear. Finally the magician becomes furious. He grabs a huge scimitar, grips it between his teeth and climbs the rope, until, like the boy, he is lost from sight.

Suddenly the air is filled with screams, and something that looks like a severed hand drops from the sky. More body parts fall as the crowd looks on in horror.

Down the rope comes the smiling magician. When he gets to the bottom, he throws his cloak over the pile of remains. Then he removes the cloak, and there stands the boy fully restored to life. The magician gives the rope a tug, the ball falls from the sky, and the magician and his assistant bow to the applauding audience.

Though the trick sounds like an Arabian Nights fable, a number of credible witnesses had reported seeing it performed. Here's how it's done:

The most important thing to know is that the Indian rope trick can be performed only at night, in an area poorly lit by torches. Before the performance, the magician strings a wire between two trees. In the dark the wire is invisible.

Once the performance starts, the torches only illuminate an area a few feet above the ground. The ball actually contains a hook, and when the magician tosses it in the air, the hook catches on the wire, and it looks as if the ball has disappeared and the rope is standing upright on its own.

As the boy climbs the rope he passes from the lighted area to the dark, and the spectators can no longer see him. He is able to balance himself on the wire. Traditionally the magicians were also acrobats. The magician himself does the same. Before climbing the rope the magician conceals pieces of a dead monkey under his cloak. He drops these to the ground once he is out of sight of the crowd. When he comes down the rope he has the boy hidden beneath the cloak, and in a big finish the boy appears from under the cloak.

While an illusion like this would not work in a modern well-lit arena, it could be quite effective in a torchlit marketplace.

Eastern magicians had a number of variations on the rope

trick; usually the magician appeared to be supported by a piece of rope or other insubstantial object. There is nothing supernatural about such feats; they are illusions like the "floating woman" illusion, which is common in many western magic shows.

THE GREAT DYING

Today, practically everyone knows that the dinosaurs died off suddenly and mysteriously sixty-five million years ago. The cause of this mass extinction has been endlessly speculated on. Currently, the most popular theory is that an asteroid or comet struck the Earth, setting off a series of worldwide catastrophes that led to the death of the dinosaurs and a lot of other animals.

While the death of the dinosaurs at the end of the geological period called the Cretaceous is the best-known episode of mass extinction, it is far from the only one in the history of the Earth. And it is by no means the most severe. In fact, the Cretaceous extinctions only rank fifth on the list of mass extinctions.

A quarter of a billion years ago, at the end of the period known as the Permian, up to ninety-six percent of the plant and animal species on Earth were wiped out. That was the greatest of all global catastrophes in the history of life on this planet. The Earth was swept clean of ferocious reptile carnivores living on land, giant amphibians living on land and in the water and trilobites living so abundantly in the seas. Of all the extinctions, that of the trilobites is probably the most surprising. These crea-

Sixty-five million years ago the dinosaurs, which had been the dominant form of life on earth, all died out suddenly and mysteriously.

tures, which resemble no creature alive today, had been the dominant marine species for millions upon millions of years. Fossils of trilobites are among the most common found in ancient rocks. Yet after the end of the Permian, 250 million years ago, they were suddenly all gone.

In 1992 scientists presented evidence that the Permian extinctions were the result of a monstrous volcanic eruption that covered much of Siberia with molten rock, touching off an ice age and a worldwide deluge of lethal acid rain.

But this theory—in fact all theories about mass extinctions— remains controversial. Some scientists believe that all the periods of mass extinction were triggered by asteroid or comet impacts. Some have suggested that the great volcanic eruptions at the end of the Permian were set off by an impact with a large celestial object. Others say the impacts counted for very little and even the extinction of the dinosaurs cannot be blamed on a comet or an asteroid.

All we can say for certain is that the history of life on Earth has been far more violent and catastrophic than we had previously imagined.

THE MYSTERIOUS AIRSHIP

On December 17, 1903, the Wright Brothers made their historic first flight in a powered aircraft at Kitty Hawk, North Carolina. But years earlier the nation had been swept with reports of a "mysterious airship," perhaps built by some unknown inventor.

The stories began in November 1896 and lasted until about May 1897. During that period, thousands, perhaps tens of thousands, of witnesses reported seeing the airship. The sightings started in California and slowly moved east to Ohio and West Virginia. The airship was seen over cities such as Sacramento, Omaha and Chicago. Nothing in known aviation history can account for the wave of sightings. They truly represent a nineteenth-century UFO case.

A fairly typical report was published in *The Chicago Times Herald* in April 1897. Robert Lowen, looking through field glasses, was "able to discern four lights a short distance apart and moving in unison. The first was a bright white light and appeared to be operated like a searchlight. Behind it was a green light and further to the rear were green and white lights strung together."

The *Chicago Tribune* reported: "At several points the moving wonder was observed by persons equipped with small telescopes or powerful field glasses, and those persons claim to have described the outlines of a structure bearing the lights. The consensus of judgment ... is that the main body of the night flyer was about seventy feet in length of slender proportions and fragile constructions. ... A few observers claim that they also saw, a short distance above the body, lateral structures resembling wings or sails."

In other cases witnesses said they had actually seen the airship land and had met the mysterious inventor and his crew, though they were never satisfactorily identified. Wilder tales hinted that the airship came from another planet, and one widely circulated story held that a spaceship crashed in Aurora, Texas, in 1897. The body of the alien killed in the crash is supposed to be buried in the Aurora Cemetery, though no one is exactly sure where.

Airship stories were an enormous sensation throughout the United States, and they were regularly reported in Europe as well. Then, just as suddenly as they started, the stories ended, and the entire phenomenon was completely forgotten. It wasn't

A drawing supposedly made from a photograph of the mysterious airship when it appeared over Chicago on April 11, 1897. (Chicago Historical Society)

until the 1960s that UFO researchers, rummaging through old newspapers, rediscovered the wave of sightings.

It is impossible to determine exactly what happened. Undoubtedly, plenty of the reports were newspaper hoaxes. Late nineteenth-century newspapermen regarded the journalistic hoax as a legitimate art form. In some cases, tricksters released lighted balloons. There is also some evidence that railroad telegraph operators were engaged in an informal conspiracy to spread airship stories.

The public knew that inventors were already at work on heavier-than-air flying machines at the time, and it was expected that one day soon one would be developed. Once stories began appearing in the newspapers, many people doubtless began misinterpreting ordinary phenomena like meteors and bright planets as the lights of an airship.

But beneath all the mistakes and hoaxes, there may be some genuinely mysterious events.

CRASHED SAUCERS

Ever since 1947, when the modern era of interest in UFOs began, rumors have circulated that a flying saucer (as UFOs were called at first) had crashed, somewhere in the American Southwest, and that the wreckage and the craft's alien crew, who were killed, had been retrieved by the U.S. government. The wreckage was stored in an elaborately guarded hangar at some U.S. Air Force base, and the bodies of the aliens were being kept there in cold storage. The government was covering up news of this astonishing event, presumably because such news would panic the public.

The rumor first received wide publicity in a 1950 book, *Behind the Flying Saucers,* by Frank Scully, a former writer for the show-business paper *Variety.* This was one of the very first of the UFO books. It turned out that Scully's information had come from a couple of notorious con men, and the book was thoroughly discredited. However, the rumors of the crashed saucer refused to die.

Later rumors circulated that President Dwight Eisenhower himself visited the secret hangar in which the remains of the spaceship were stored in 1954. An even more bizarre variation of this rumor was that spaceships had landed at Edwards Air Force Base in California in 1954 and that Eisenhower went there to meet with the aliens.

The rumors surfaced once again in the 1980s. This time a couple of UFO researchers said they had a document indicating the existence of a super secret group of scientists and government officials who had been in charge of operating the cover-up. There was also a letter signed by President Harry Truman about a meeting of this secret group. These documents created a great deal of excitement in UFO circles for many months, but now both are widely (though not universally) assumed to be fakes.

All of these stories and rumors appear to have started with a real event. On July 2, 1947, something landed or crashed on a remote ranch near Rosewell, New Mexico. Investigators from a local air force base visited the ranch to view the debris. The initial press release issued by the Rosewell base was sensational. It said that "a flying disc" had landed and "action was immediately taken and the disc was picked up at the rancher's home. It was inspected at the Rosewell Army Air Field and subsequently loaned by Major (Jesse A.) Marcel to higher headquarters."

That release was picked up by newspapers all over the world. It was almost immediately revised by air force spokesmen who said that the flying disc was nothing more than a downed weather balloon.

But UFO investigators during the 1980s interviewed many who had been connected with the original incident—though the most important witnesses had long since died. These investigators have concluded that a good deal more than a weather balloon crashed at Rosewell that July day.

Other investigators have pursued the theory of a massive government cover-up by trying to gain release of official documents from the 1940s. So far they have uncovered nothing even remotely resembling a smoking gun. But the hunt goes on.

THE PHILADELPHIA EXPERIMENT

For many years, a rumor has persisted that sometime during World War II the U.S. Navy conducted a successful test of teleportation. The S.S. *Andrew Fursenth* was transported instantly from its dock in Philadelphia to a dock in the Norfolk, Newport News, and Portsmouth areas and back again. The teleportation lasted only a few minutes, but the experiment had such puzzling and disastrous long-term effects that the whole thing was covered up.

According to the story, half the crew was lost. Many of the survivors were "mad as hatters." Others would "go blank" or "get stuck." They would seem to disappear or "freeze" on the spot.

This incredible tale first came to light in a UFO book written in 1955 by Maurice K. Jessup, an astronomer with an interest in UFOs. The following year the report received confirmation of sorts in a series of strange rambling letters written by a man calling himself Carlos Allende or Carl Allen. The writer claimed that he had actually witnessed the experiment.

On April 29, 1959, Maurice Jessup was found dead inside his car in a Dade County, Florida, park. The verdict was suicide. Some insist that Jessup was actually murdered because he "knew too much" about the Philadelphia Experiment. Those who knew Jessup, however, say he was a deeply troubled man who had often talked of suicide.

The man who was almost certainly the real Carlos Allende

showed up at the headquarters of a UFO group and confessed that his letters had been a hoax, that he had written "because Jessup's writings scared me." Later he tried to retract his confession. Those who have met Allende tend to dismiss him as a harmless eccentric, one who should not be taken seriously.

It is possible that the whole idea of the Philadelphia Experiment began with real experiments in "degaussing"—neutralizing—a ship's magnetism so that it could pass over magnetic mines without setting them off. A degaussed ship would, in a sense, disappear—but only magnetically; the physical body of the ship would, of course, stay where it was. Jessup and/or Allende may have heard of these experiments and become confused or decided they were just a cover-up for far more sensational work on teleportation.

Despite the slender, nearly nonexistent evidence for the Philadelphia Experiment, it has become part of our folklore. References to it appear regularly in books of "mysteries," and it was even the basis for a film.

PREHISTORIC BRAIN SURGERY

Even today brain surgery is considered one of the most difficult and dangerous medical procedures. Yet there is considerable evidence that some form of brain surgery was widely practiced in ancient times and that a surprisingly large number of the patients survived.

Archaeologists had discovered many ancient human skulls with holes cut in them. It was assumed that the holes had been cut after death for some magical or religious purpose. But in the late nineteenth century scientists began taking a closer look at some of these skulls and found evidence that the holes had not been cut after death, but before, and in many cases the bone around the hole had begun to regrow, showing that the patient had not only been alive, but had survived for a considerable period of time.

The operation of cutting a hole in the skull is called trephination. Trepanned skulls turned up among skulls from Stone Age Europe to ancient Peru. It was the Peruvian Indians who apparently made most extensive use of this operation. The trepanned skulls of Peru are mostly those of adult males who had suffered other head injuries. Perhaps they were warriors wounded by clubs or missiles from slings. The hole in the skull may have been used to reduce pressure on the brain from swelling or to remove fragments of bone. It is less clear what the ancient Europeans used the operation for. It may have been used in cases of mental illness where cutting a hole in the skull seemed a logical way of releasing the demons that seemed to have possessed the brain. By the fifth century B.C. Greek physicians used the operation to help treat head injuries, as the Peruvians did.

About 50 percent of the trepanned Peruvian skulls indicate that the patients survived. That was a better survival rate than that of early twentieth-century brain surgeons. And remember that most of the ancient Peruvian patients were already badly wounded and thus went into surgery in a weakened condition. Fully 75 percent of those who underwent trephination in the early twentieth century died, usually from infection. It is possible that ancient surgeons did not have to contend with infectious organisms as virulent as those in the modern world.

THE HOLY GRAIL

From ancient times to modern Hollywood, the quest for the Holy Grail has been one of the most frequently retold stories. The story, however, is not in the Bible. In fact, it was not even originally a Christian story.

The legend probably originated in Celtic mythology with its tales of magic "vessels of plenty" that provide limitless food and drink. When the story was adapted by medieval Christian writers, the grail became either the cup from which Christ drank at the Last Supper or the chalice in which the blood of the crucified Christ was collected.

In one version of the legend, the grail came into the possession of Joseph of Arimathea, the merchant who provided the tomb for Jesus. After the Crucifixion, Joseph made his way to Britain and settled in Glastonbury, where he established Britain's first Christian community. According to tradition he put the grail in an ancient well, now known as Chalice Well. It is said to never run dry. Ruins of a magnificent abbey are located in Glastonbury, and the area had long contained a Christian religious community. But it does not go back to the days of Joseph of Arimathea. Still thousands of pilgrims go to Glastonbury every year to view Chalice Well.

It is not the grail itself but the search for the grail that has held the greatest fascination over the centuries. The story has been retold in countless romances dating back to at least the twelfth century. The most famous of these is associated with King Arthur, whose castle at Camelot was believed by some to be near Glastonbury. The best known of the many Arthur stories is Thomas Malory's *Le Morte d'Arthur,* written in the fifteenth century.

In Malory's account, a vision of the Holy Grail appears before Arthur's Knights of the Round Table. The knights then vow to find the grail and bring it to Camelot. The quest is marked by all sorts of magical and mystic events.

Since the grail is more a spiritual object than a material one, it can be possessed only by the purest of knights. That eliminated the bravest knight, Lancelot, because of his illicit love for Queen Guinevere.

THE CRYSTAL SKULL

A beautifully fashioned skull made from quartz crystal has been the object of much speculation and some wild stories. People have reported hearing strange noises around the skull. Objects are said to have been mysteriously moved in its presence. People who scoffed at the skull's powers have reputedly been struck dead.

The powers attributed to the skull are doubtful, but the mystery and controversy surrounding it are quite real.

The skull was first brought to the world's attention in the 1950s by British traveler and adventurer F. A. Mitchell-Hedges, who said it had been found at a Mayan site in Honduras. Unfortunately, Mitchell-Hedges had a well-deserved reputation for making up romantic tales, and this seems to have been one of them. He apparently bought the skull at an art auction in Lon-

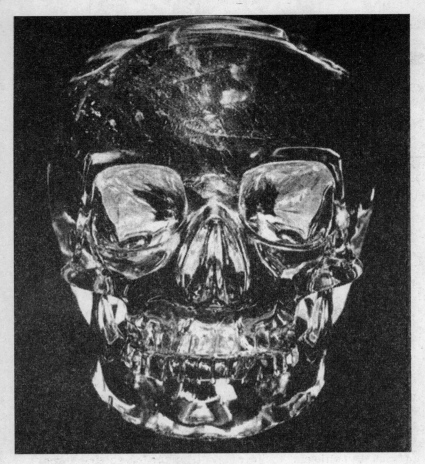

The mysterious crystal skull.

don in 1944. The previous owner had been an art dealer, and prior to that it had been in a private collection.

But this does not dispel the mystery of the skull's origins. It is a wonderful piece of work, weighing eleven pounds and cut from a block of quartz crystal, apparently without the use of any machine tools.

The skull was a common motif in Aztec or Mixtec art and several small skulls of crystal have been found in Mexico. This skull is larger and far more anatomically correct than the Mexican specimens. According to one authority: "Such realism seems beyond the ordinary range of Aztec art, and gives the skull the character almost of an anatomic study in a scientific age."

Another authority suggested it might be a memento mori (a reminder of death) of sixteenth- to eighteenth-century origin. It might have been made in China for a European client.

The crystal skull still fascinates and puzzles all who examine it.

THE CABALA

Cabala is a Hebrew word meaning "that which is received or tradition." What is usually called the Cabala is a body of mystical thought and writings that was organized in Jewish communities in southern France and Spain in the twelfth and thirteenth centuries. It continued to grow and develop for another three hundred years. The principal work of the Jewish Cabala is *Zohar,* or *Book of Splendor.* It was written somewhere around the year 1280 by the scholar Moses de Leon.

Like all mystical books, *Zohar* is extremely difficult for the nonmystic to understand. It has been said that no man who has immersed himself in the study of it has ever emerged entirely sane.

In the Cabala, as in other mystical systems, there is secrecy.

The mystics fear if their special knowledge is given to the ignorant and uninitiated it will either be misinterpreted or misused. Therefore, already obscure ideas are often made deliberately more difficult. The "true meaning" or "inner meaning" of the doctrines is kept secret and revealed only to those who have undergone a long period of study and testing.

Cabalistic mysticism has never been in the mainstream of Judaism. Indeed, many Jewish scholars are deeply suspicious of it. The theory places great emphasis on the power of certain words and numbers. Another element of cabalistic tradition is that things are not what they seem and that a hidden meaning can be found in everything.

Among simpler folk, the scholarly cabalists, preoccupied with words and numbers and secret and mysterious in their way of life, had a reputation for being magicians. People began wearing charms inscribed with cabalistic names and symbols. The amulets were aimed at everything from protecting the wearer from the evil eye to producing invisibility.

By the fifteenth century some Christians began to develop an interest in the Cabala. At first they attempted to prove that the truth of Christianity was the hidden meaning behind the Cabala. Later, what they believed to be the magical possibilities of the Cabala became most important.

By the seventeenth century the original Cabala was almost lost entirely among those Christians who claimed to be students of the doctrines. The word *Cabala* increasingly became a term to describe any kind of secret and obscure magical lore.

The Cabala picked up a more dangerous association. Because of its secrecy, the Cabala became synonymous with plot or intrigue. The word *cabal,* which means "a secret group gathered together for some sinister purpose," comes from *Cabala.*

THE MISSING BONES

One of the greatest discoveries in the history of human paleontology was made in a large cave near the village of Choukoutien about twenty-five miles from the capital of China, which was called Peking by Westerners. The cave yielded the remains of about forty early humans who were given the popular name Peking Man, plus tools and other evidence of human habitation. No find of the fossil remains of early humans before, or since, has been remotely as rich as this one. The fossils were taken to the Peking Union Medical College for study.

But the discovery was made during the 1930s, a time when war threatened to engulf all of Asia. The Japanese had already invaded parts of China, and Chinese authorities were afraid that the scientific treasure might fall into the hands of the invaders.

In 1941 it was arranged to have the bones of Peking Man taken out of China secretly and brought to the United States for safekeeping. They were crated up to be shipped by train to the port city of Chinwangtao, where they were to be put aboard an American steamship.

But the authorities had waited too long for the plan to be carried out. The United States and Japan were already at war. The train was intercepted, and the marines captured. And the boxes containing the bones simply disappeared.

Many believed that the Japanese had taken the fossils back to Japan. But after the war, no trace of them could be found anywhere in Japan, and nothing indicates that the Japanese soldiers who stopped the train had any idea what was in the boxes. They may have considered them of no value and simply discarded them. Or they could have been put into a warehouse that was later bombed or looted. If the boxes had contained gold, a simple soldier would have recognized their value—but what would he have made of fragments of bone? How could he have guessed that the boxes contained a treasure infinitely more valuable than gold?

One story related that after the war the bones had been smuggled out of China by a U.S. serviceman. After he died, someone who had known him was trying to either sell the bones or return them. However, the person who claimed to be in possession of the bones was never able to provide adequate proof, and nothing ever resulted. Other equally unverifiable rumors have circulated about the location of the Peking Man's remains.

Most people knowledgeable about the events surrounding the disappearance of the bones believe they were destroyed. When war threatened, casts and careful drawings of the bones were made and sent out of China. But they can never replace the bones themselves. And so, despite the almost infinitesimal chance of finding them, the search for the bones of Peking Man is sure to continue.

INCA GOLD

In 1532 the Spanish conquistador Pizarro invited the Inca emperor Atahualpa to what was supposed to be a peaceful meeting. But the treacherous Pizarro had prepared a trap, and the Inca ruler was captured and imprisoned.

To gain his freedom, Atahualpa offered a ransom of enough gold to fill his prison chamber. It was said to be a room measuring twenty-two feet long and seventeen feet wide, and the Inca promised it would be filled to a level of about eight feet. The emperor also promised to fill another room twice over with silver.

Pizarro was delighted and agreed. Immediately, runners went out to all parts of the great Inca empire, delivering the message that all available gold must be gathered to pay the king's ransom. Golden artifacts were stripped from palaces and temples, loaded on llamas and sent to the city of Cuzco where the emperor was being held. The Spaniards melted down the treasures and got about twenty tons of gold and silver bars.

But Pizarro never intended to free the Inca ruler. He feared, with good reason, that Atahualpa would then lead his people against the small band of conquerors. So he had the Inca executed.

As soon as word of the emperor's death spread, the caravans of gold and silver heading toward Cuzco stopped. Vast quantities of treasure were hidden from the invaders. The Spanish were able to find some, but an unknown quantity of golden treasure still may remain hidden throughout the old Inca empire. One Inca nobleman said, "That which the Inca gave to the Spaniards was but a kernel of corn compared with the heap before him."

For centuries, treasure hunters and archaeologists have searched for the missing Inca gold, without success.

THINGS FROM THE SKY

The eccentric American writer Charles Hoy Fort liked to collect odd bits of information about things that shouldn't have happened but did. He put all of these bits and pieces together in several books that are still popular today. Practically any odd or unexplained happening is now called *Fortean*. This was a word coined by admirers of the writer.

One of the things that most fascinated Fort were the tales of things—frogs, fish, blocks of ice, seeds or whatever—that mysteriously fell out of the sky. Of frogs from the sky he wrote:

"Tremendous number of little toads, one or two months old, that were seen to fall from a great thick cloud that appeared suddenly in a sky that had been cloudless, August 1804, near Toulouse, France, according to a letter from Prof. Pontus to M. Argo.

"Many instances of frogs that were seen to fall from the sky. Accounts of such falls, signed by witnesses.

"A shower of frogs which darkened the air and covered the

ground for a long distance is reported as the result of a recent rainstorm in Kansas City, Mo.''

Frog falls, however, are not nearly as numerous as fish falls. The sixteenth-century Swedish ecclesiastic and writer Olaus Magnus told of many such events in his history of Scandinavia.

One of the best-known fish falls occurred at Mountain Ash in a valley in Wales, on February 11, 1859. The fish fell over a very limited area for about two minutes. Many were still alive, and they were sent to the British Museum for examination. They were of two types, minnows and sticklebacks. The surviving fish were exhibited at the Zoological Garden in Regent's Park.

According to Fort, a number of speckled snakes fell from the sky into the streets of Hathorne, Massachusetts, after a thunderstorm. During July 1822 great quantities of seeds of unknown origin fell in various parts of Germany. Fort and other oddity collectors have also recorded stories of hay or straw and large chunks of ice falling mysteriously from the sky.

There can be no single explanation for all these mysterious falls. Some of the stories are undoubtedly hoaxes or at least exaggerations. Frogs and fish might have been carried a short distance in a waterspout or moved by some other weather phenomenon. But more unrestrained speculators have suggested that at least some of these things from the sky may be dropped out of another universe or another dimension.

AMERICAN ELEPHANTS

Mammoths and mastodons, close relatives of the modern elephant, were once numerous in North America and South America. Thomas Jefferson, who had one of the best scientific minds in the America of his day, examined mammoth bones found in his native Virginia. Though no one in Virginia had ever seen a living mammoth, Jefferson was convinced that they still roamed the then unexplored territory to the west. Jefferson, and most of his contemporaries, did not believe that species could become extinct.

No mammoths were ever found, and the world realized that species do indeed become extinct. Most scientists then assumed that man and elephant had never shared the American continents together, that the elephants had died off long before human beings had arrived.

That assumption held up until the early years of this century when unmistakable evidence was found that humans and mammoths were not only contemporaries, but that mammoths were widely hunted.

But when did the mammoths and mastodons die out? Did the later American Indians retain a memory of these elephantlike creatures? Indeed, was it possible that a few ancient elephants survived at the time the Europeans came to America?

Everything from Mayan carvings to Midwestern Indian mounds have been cited as evidence that the Indians either knew or remembered the elephantlike creatures their ancestors

The Mayan carving shows what may be elephants or birds called "macaws." Note the nostril at the top of the "trunk" and what appears to be feathers surrounding a large round eye. (*From Ancient Ruins and Archaeology*)

had hunted. However, all of this physical evidence was based on misinterpretation. Elephant carvings found inside some Indian mounds turned out to be deliberate hoaxes.

Some Indian myths and legends describe huge shaggy animals that could have been mammoths. And one story told by an English seaman named Ingram relates how he wandered around North America in 1580 and saw huge shaggy elephants being hunted by the Indians of what is now Pennsylvania.

Legends and travelers' tales are very weak evidence upon which to build a case. The most reasonable theory is that the mammoths and mastodons died out over 10,000 years ago, and the Indians had forgotten all about them by the time Europeans arrived. But it would be foolish to be dogmatic on this point, for not so long ago the practically unanimous scientific opinion was that humans and elephants did not coexist in the Americas, and that opinion was wrong.

MISSING NAZI GOLD

Before they were defeated, the Nazis had systematically looted the countries they conquered. The gold reserves of the conquered nations were particular targets. Much of the stolen gold was stored in vaults of Berlin's Reichsbank.

By February 1945 Germany was on the brink of final defeat. Allied air raids had nearly destroyed the walls of the bank. Hitler's officials shipped the bank's reserves of gold and paper money to a mine some 200 miles southwest of Berlin. But within a few weeks, the area was occupied by allied troops who found most of the money and gold.

The crumbling Nazi regime then tried to consolidate what was left of the bank's reserves from branch offices in Berlin. Then it was to be shipped to Munich and distributed to Reichsbank branches in southern Germany. Two special trains carried the gold.

Hitler killed himself in his Berlin bunker on April 30, and after that the disintegration of Nazi power accelerated. Much of the gold was stolen by those who were supposed to be guarding it. Gold was hidden in caves and buried in fields.

On May 15 the Russians took control of what remained of

the Reichsbank, including some $3 million in gold bullion, which vanished.

So much confusion reigned that there never was, and never could be, an accurate accounting of the bank's assets. But it is assumed that at least $2 billion in gold, and perhaps a lot more, remains unaccounted for. Much of it was probably hidden in the hills of southern Germany. And much of what was hidden was probably found by Nazis who knew where it had been stashed, by Allied soldiers who stumbled on it or by ordinary Germans, none of whom would have reported their finds.

But a fortune in gold—maybe several fortunes—may still remain hidden.

THE *TITANIC* PROPHECY

What has been called "the most astounding instance of prophecy" is to be found in a novel. In 1898 a book called *The Wreck of the Titan,* by a virtually unknown writer named Morgan Robertson, was published. It was a disaster novel about the sinking of a great ocean liner, but the book was not a success.

In 1912, fourteen years after the publication of *The Wreck of the Titan,* the events described in the novel came horribly and spectacularly true. The *Titanic,* the largest, most luxurious ocean liner ever built, struck an iceberg and sank in the greatest civilian naval tragedy in history.

The parallels between the novel and the real events are truly startling. First, there are the names of the ships, *Titan* and *Titanic.* Both were on their maiden voyages across the Atlantic.

75 FEET FROM BOAT DECK TO WATER.

Passengers abandoning ship after the *Titanic* struck an iceberg.

Both were triple-screw vessels, and both had an inadequate number of life boats: twenty-four on the *Titan* and only twenty on the *Titanic*. The *Titan* was a 70,000-ton ship; the *Titanic* was a 66,000-ton ship. Both sank in April after hitting an iceberg in the North Atlantic with an appalling loss of life. Most of the 2,300 on the *Titan* and 1,503 of the 2,206 on the *Titanic* died. Both ships had been described as "unsinkable." In the novel, one of the characters says, "God Himself could not sink the ship." The *Titanic*'s owners, the White Star Line, had declared her to be absolutely safe. She had sixteen watertight compartments, and even if the first four were torn open, she could easily stay afloat.

Prophecy? Well, perhaps, but the author, who seems to have known a good deal about ocean liners, may simply have been writing about realistic dangers. Icebergs were a recognized danger to ships in the North Atlantic, and April was the month when the iceberg danger was greatest. As for the names *Titan* and *Titanic*—both meant "huge," and the liners were meant to be that. It may have been a lucky, or unlucky, guess. The author of *The Wreck of the Titan* never appears to have claimed any prophetic powers. The way in which reality seems to have followed fiction may have been a coincidence, though admittedly a remarkable one.

TREASURE TROVES OF FACT-FILLED FUN FROM AVON CAMELOT

HOW TO TRAVEL THROUGH TIME
by James M. Deem   76681-7/ $3.50 US/ $4.50 CAN

HOW TO CATCH A FLYING SAUCER
by James M. Deem   71898-7/ $3.50 US/ $4.50 CAN

HOW TO HUNT BURIED TREASURE
by James M. Deem   72176-7/ $3.99 US/ $4.99 CAN

ASK ME ANYTHING ABOUT THE PRESIDENTS
by Louis Phillips   76426-1/ $3.99 US/ $4.99 CAN

KID CAMPING FROM AAAIII! TO ZIP
by Patrick F. McManus   71311-X/ $3.50 US/ $4.25 CAN

EXPLORING AUTUMN
by Sandra Markle   71910-X/ $3.50 US/ $4.50 CAN

GOBBLE! THE COMPLETE BOOK OF THANKSGIVING WORDS
by Lynda Graham-Barber   71963-0/ $3.99 US/ $4.99 CAN